ACTION AND AD

Skill-Oriented Language A

Written by Judith B. Steffens and Judy F. Carr
Illustrated by Beverly Armstrong

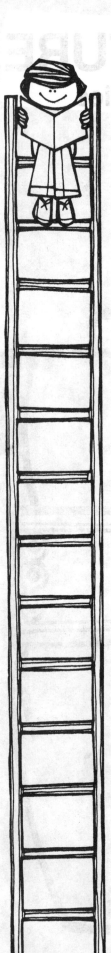

The Learning Works

Edited by Sherri René Butterfield

The purchase of this book entitles the individual teacher to reproduce copies for use in the classroom.

The reproduction of any part for an entire school or school system or for commercial use is strictly prohibited.

No form of this work may be reproduced or transmitted or recorded without written permission from the publisher.

Contents

Contents
(continued)

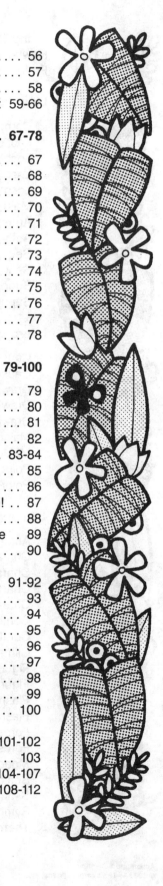

To the Teacher

Action and Adventure is a skill-oriented, thematic language arts unit with great appeal for adolescents. It casts individual and group reading skill lessons in a framework of action, adventure, and excitement.

Action and Adventure is divided into five sections: Literal Comprehension, Interpretive Comprehension, Literary Terms, Vocabulary, and Skill Stretchers.

Literal Comprehension includes skill lessons and activities covering compare and contrast, fact or opinion, locating specific information, identifying supporting details, recognizing the main idea, understanding the author's purpose, and sequencing.

Interpretive Comprehension includes skill lessons and activities covering cause and effect, drawing conclusions, making inferences, and point of view.

Literary Terms includes skill lessons and activities covering antagonist/protagonist, characterization, climax, conflict, figurative language, flashback, foreshadowing, mood, setting, symbol, theme, and tone.

Vocabulary includes skill lessons and activities covering analogies, connotation/denotation, context clues, dictionary skills, homonyms, multiple meanings, prefixes, suffixes, synonyms, and use of the thesaurus.

Skill Stretchers includes imaginative formats for student book reports and clever ideas for game, puzzle, dramatization, and creative writing activities designed to reinforce or enrich the reading and language arts skills taught in this unit.

You may use these activities in the order presented or select specific ones to match your students' diagnosed skill development needs. To aid you in making such selections, each activity has been identified by both skill and title in the table of contents. A boxed explanation or definition with examples is provided for each term or concept introduced. Also provided are a bibliography of action and adventure literature appropriate for junior and senior high students, a pretest and a posttest for measuring student progress, and an answer key for the tests and for all of the activities that are not open-ended.

Action and Adventure may be used as an independent unit with both homogeneous and heterogeneous classes, as an enrichment unit, as a source of individual skill lessons, or as a supplement to any basal text.

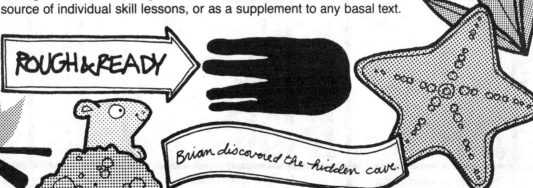

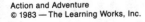

How to Use This Book

The skill sheets, group activities, and individual activity sheets included in this book can be used in many ways.

	Day 1	Day 2	Day 3	Day 4	Day 5
Homogeneous Group	Group activity to introduce skill. Assign story to class to be finished as homework.	Individual skill sheet. Review individual skill sheet. Check understanding and application of the concept, term, or skill.	Vocabulary—either a general lesson or a lesson related to the story read. Record vocabulary in notebook. Review and collect skill sheets.	Follow-up skill lesson directly related to story. Review skill lesson with class. Collect, correct, and save skill lesson.	Enrichment Day. Independent novel reading *or* Individual activity sheet *or* Group activity.
Heterogeneous Group	Group activity to introduce skill. Either assign three levels of the same story or three different stories of differing reading levels to be finished as homework.	Individual skill lesson for entire class. Confer with Group A to discuss story while Groups B and C complete skill lesson and begin vocabulary work.	Confer with Group B while Group C completes vocabulary work. Confer with Group C while Groups A and B complete vocabulary work.	Follow-up lesson directly related to story. Use one lesson applicable to all three stories or create a separate follow-up lesson for each story.	Enrichment Day. Story sharing *or* Independent novel reading *or* Individual activity sheet *or* Group activity.
Basal Reader	Use individual skill sheet and group activity ideas to introduce and reinforce skills found in the reading assignments.				
Notes	1. Assign an independent novel as part of each reading unit. 2. Give quizzes as needed to hold student interest and check progress. 3. Use individual activity sheets for optional enrichment or as required assignments. 4. Use the Reading Skills Checklist on page 103 to keep a record of the reading skills students have mastered and those that need additional reinforcement.				

Pretest

Read the excerpt below.

Sara's strong arms strained as she tried to move against the undulating sea. "I'm going to win!" she repeated determinedly to herself. She thought with anger of her coach, Lou Jenkins. How could she have admired that man? He was like a mother cat, always overprotecting his athletes. Well, she wasn't going to be mothered. He'd said she was headstrong and unpredictable; he just didn't seem to understand that, as the defending champion, she had a responsibility to compete.

The tape cutting into her ankle was a less-than-subtle reminder of just how close she had come to missing the Kohoa Surfing Classic. Sara shook her head as she remembered her own foolishness. She'd practiced with caution all week, but yesterday her need for fun and excitement had gotten the better of her. While she was executing a turn, a wave had caught her, and she'd been thrown from her board and dragged to the bottom. Doctor Carson said she had come close to needing surgery. Fortunately, though, her folly had resulted in nothing more than painful lacerations. And if Coach Jenkins thought a few deep scratches would stop her, he was wrong, dead wrong.

Finally, Sara had paddled out far enough. A huge wave was coming toward her. For good luck, she rubbed her hand across the palm trees painted on her surfboard. "Here goes," thought Sara. She drew her feet beneath her, found her balance, and was just about to stand up when a sharp pain seized her.

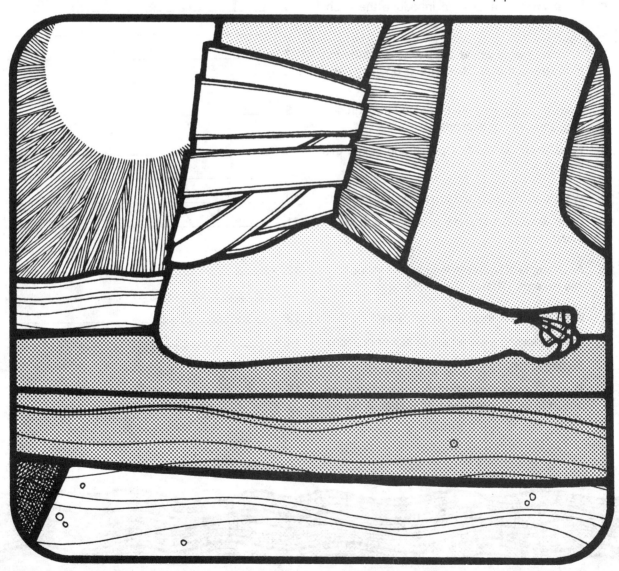

Pretest
(continued)

Read each question below. Then write the correct answer on the numbered line.

1. Who is the main character in the story?

2. From what point of view is the story told?

3. What is the setting of the story?

4. This passage contains a flashback. If you numbered the story events in the order in which they actually occurred, which event would come first?

5. Which event would come last?

6. What words are used to introduce the flashback?

7. What one word would you use to describe the mood the author creates in these opening paragraphs?

8. Does the author create this mood through setting, situation, or description?

9. What words in the first paragraph signal this mood?

10. What kind of conflict did you find in this excerpt?

11. What words foreshadow a coming change in mood or action?

12. An example of figurative language is included in this excerpt. What is it?

13. What symbol is included in the story?

14. Is the following a statement of fact or opinion?

    Surfing is fun.

15-17. The author uses three techniques of characterization to develop the main character. What are they?

1. _____

2. _____

3. _____

4. _____
   _____

5. _____
   _____

6. _____
   _____

7. _____

8. _____

9. _____
   _____

10. _____

11. _____
    _____

12. _____
    _____

13. _____

14. _____

15. _____

16. _____

17. _____
    _____

Pretest
(continued)

18. What caused Sara to fall?

18. _____

19. What was one result of the fall?

19. _____

20. Do you think Sara will win the competition? Why or why not?

20. _____
_____

21-22. Compare Sara and Coach Jenkins. What two similarities do you find?

21. _____

22. _____

23-24. What two major differences do you find?

23. _____
_____
_____
_____

24. _____
_____
_____

25. When an author writes a story, the primary purpose can be to inform, to persuade, or to entertain. What was the author's purpose in writing this story?

25. _____

26. Complete the following analogy.

A <u>wave</u> is to the <u>sea</u> as a <u>cloud</u> is to the _____.

26. _____

27-28. Write a synonym and an antonym for the word <u>strong</u>.

27. *Synonym:* _____

28. *Antonym:* _____

29. The word <u>strike</u> may mean to hit. It may also mean _____.

29. _____

30. Add a root word or a base word to the suffix <u>-ness</u>

30. _____

31. What does the word you wrote on line 30 mean?

31. _____

32. In the word <u>rework</u>, what does the prefix mean?

32. _____

33. What kind of context clue is given in the following sentence?

She had hoped for something worthwhile, but the search proved futile.

33. _____

34. What is the denotation of the word <u>childish</u>?

34. _____
_____

35. What does the word <u>childish</u> connote?

35. _____

Name _____

Climb Aboard

> To **compare** is to show the ways in which similar things are alike or different. To **contrast** is to show the ways in which unlike things are different.

Before the advent of the train, the stagecoach provided transportation for hundreds of travelers. Here's your chance to climb aboard by comparing two replicas of Wells Fargo Stage Line tickets. You should be able to find at least five similarities and five differences.

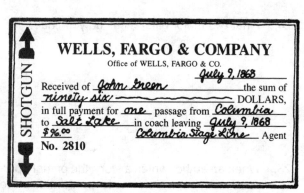

Similarities

1. Both tickets were issued to _____.

2. Both tickets were issued by _____.

3. _____.

4. _____.

5. _____.

Differences

1. The ticket on the left was issued on _____,

   while the ticket on the right was issued on_____.

2. The destination indicated for the ticket on the left is _____,

   while the destination indicated for the ticket on the right is _____.

3. _____

   _____.

4. _____

   _____.

5. _____

Name _____

"Beleve" It or Not

> A **fact** is a statement that has been or can be proved to be true.
> *Example:* Jacques-Yves Cousteau is a French oceanographer.
> An **opinion** is a statement that is believed but cannot be proved.
> *Example:* Undersea exploration is very dangerous.

The letter to the editor on page 12 contains both facts and opinions about the famous Bermuda Triangle. Read the letter and then list the facts and opinions on the lines below.

Facts

1. _____
_____
2. _____
_____
3. _____
4. _____
5. _____
_____
6. _____

Opinions

1. _____
_____
2. _____
3. _____
_____
4. _____
5. _____
_____
6. _____
_____
7. _____
8. _____

Mr. I. Beleve's letter is obviously highly opinionated. Pretend that you are the editor to whom it has been written, and write a response to it. Remember that you must stick to the facts. If you need additional information, look it up in your school or community library.

"Beleve" It or Not
(continued)

The Editor
Boats in Bottles Digest
Seaview, Iowa

Dear Sir:

I read with amazement your article regarding the Bermuda Triangle. In it, you state that "the mystery surrounding this area of the Atlantic Ocean can be easily explained away by human error or natural causes." Your smug assumption that you have all of the answers deserves a response from someone who knows better—me!

There is obviously something <u>very</u> mysterious about the waters stretching from Florida to Bermuda to Puerto Rico. Why, more than one hundred boats and planes have disappeared from there since 1930, and history textbooks are filled with accounts of unexplained disappearances in the Triangle. How do you account for the fact that in 1945, Flight 19—a group of five U.S. Navy bombers on a routine mission—vanished completely? Moreover, the rescue plane sent to look for them disappeared as well. Even if we were to assume that the planes were lost because of human error, there is no way to explain the lack of wreckage. It is apparent that, in an area as shallow and clear as the one in which the planes were last sighted, some wreckage should have been found. There are innumerable other examples as well. In 1881, for example, the *Mary Celeste* was found afloat with no crew aboard—and no indication of any disturbance. The ship was searched thoroughly, from top to bottom. Surely some indication of trouble would have been found if the disappearance had been the result of natural causes.

I could go on interminably, with accounts of boats and planes whose disappearances have never been explained. Nor will they be—even by the natural causes you cite. Clear air turbulence and magnetic variation—two of the reasons you mentioned—would certainly have been anticipated by experienced pilots and captains. These reasons simply are not sufficient to explain the continual strange reports coming from that area.

The Bermuda Triangle is, and will continue to be, a mystery.

Sincerely yours,

I. Beleve

I. Beleve

Name _____

Wanted: Action and Adventure!

If you are looking for a career that is filled with action and adventure, you may want to consider one of the following:

- archaeologist
- arctic explorer
- astronaut
- deep-sea fisherman
- espionage agent
- fire fighter
- forest ranger
- jungle explorer

- long-distance swimmer
- parachutist
- paramedic
- rescue team member
- sailor
- skin diver
- spelunker
- test pilot

Many of these careers may be appealing, but how can you decide whether or not one of them is what you're looking for? You can find out by selecting one career and researching it thoroughly to obtain answers to these six important questions.

1. What type of work is involved?
2. What basic education and specialized training are needed?
3. In what location is most of the work usually done?
4. What working conditions would you experience?
5. What special equipment would you need?
6. What unusual hazards does the job present?

Once you have completed your research, share what you have learned with others. Write an advertisement for a position in the field you have chosen. Be sure that the ad provides information to answer the questions asked above—and makes the job sound appealing. You're limited, of course, by the number of words you can afford—fifty in all!

HELP WANTED!

_____

_____

_____

_____

_____

_____

Spread the Word

Each of the well-known outlaws listed below created headaches for the lawmen of his day. Do some thorough research on one of these scoundrels. Then use the information you have gathered to create an eye-catching wanted poster in the frame provided on page 15.

The Apache Kid
Sam Bass
Charles "Black Bart" Bolton
Billy the Kid
Butch Cassidy (Robert Leroy Parker)
Cherokee Bill (Crawford Goldsby)
Bill Cook

Bob, Grat, and Emmet Dalton
Bill Doolin
John Wesley Hardin
Jesse James
Harry Longbaugh (The Sundance Kid)
The Reno Brothers
Tall Texan (Ben Kilpatrick)

WANTED
for
Murder

Max "Butch" Wiler

Alias:	Billie Maxwell	**Height:**	5′ 10″
	Butch Maxwell	**Weight:**	180 lbs.
	Willie Mack	**Hair:**	Brown
		Eyes:	Brown
		Distinguishing marks:	None

★ Considered armed and dangerous.
★ Probably accompanied by Jerry Jackson, his former partner.
★ Known to frequent saloons in the El Paso area.

Forward information to the nearest law office or to Pinkerton Detective Agency.

WANTED

Name _____

Just Morse-ing Around

Morse code is used all over the world to transmit messages quickly. Telegraph operators have no trouble deciphering the dots and dashes that make up the code. How long will it take you to decode the directions for this exercise? Remember, one slash (/) is used between letters, and two slashes (//) are used between words.

International Morse Code

a ·—	f ··—·	k —·—	p ·——·	u ··—
b —···	g ——·	l ·—··	q ——·—	v ···—
c —·—·	h ····	m ——	r ·—·	w ·——
d —··	i ··	n —·	s ···	x —··—
e ·	j ·———	o ———	t —	y —·——
				z ——··

——·/·/—/·—//·—·/·/·—/—··/·—·——//—/———//···/·/—·/·—··//—//——·/—·/—·/

·—··/·——·//·—··/———/—·//····/·/·—·/·—·/———//

_____

·—·/·/·—/—·//·—/—··/···/———/·—/—··/—//·—/···//···/····/·/·/·—·/·—·——//

—··/··/·—·/·—/—·/·/·—·/·—/—··//

_____

—/····/·/—/··——/——·/—//·—/····/·/·—··/·—/—·/·—·/·—·/—/·//···/····/·/·/·—·——//———/·—·//

·——·/·—/——·/·/·—··//·—/—·/—·/···/·—·/·—·/·—·/——//——·/·/·—·/·—·/···/—·/—·//—/··—·/·/·—···

···/·/·—·/——·/·—·/·—·——//—·/·—/—·/·/·—/·—·/———//——·/—·/·/·—·/·/—·//—·/·—··/·/—/·—//———

···—/··/—·/—//·—··/·/··—/·—·/—/·—//—·/—·/—/·—·/·—·/—·//——·/·/·—·/—·/·—··/———/·—·/——/

_____

_____

Remember, the ship was sinking fast. The frantic radio operator had time to send no more than twenty-five words.

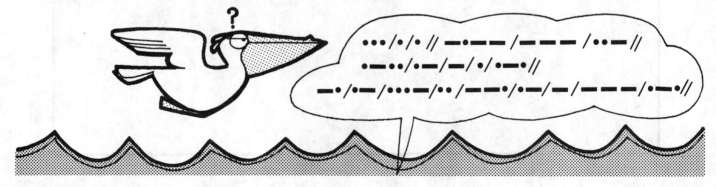

A Purposeful Discovery

> The **author's purpose** is his or her intent in writing a piece of prose or poetry.

Gawn Deagen, the noted archaeologist, sent the report below to his colleagues at the London Archaeological Society. His purpose was to inform them of a recent archaeological find. The audience for which his report was intended was a learned one, made up of other professional archaeologists. Read what Mr. Deagen wrote, then turn to page 18.

August 18, 19—

TO: Members of the London Archaeological Society
FROM: Gawn Deagen *G.D.*
RE: Recent excavations in Norway

Arrived on site in Olsag, Norway, on April 15, 19—. Prior approval to excavate the 15-foot high tumulus had been granted in January of that year.

Excavation began, and the first discovery was the prow of a vessel later determined to have been approximately 65 feet in length. Vessel had been buried in blue-gray clay, accounting for the excellent state of preservation. Remains have not yet been carbon-dated, but my feeling is that they date from approximately A.D. 825.

Continued to remove clay, and discovered that the ship was, in fact, largely intact, with huge horizontal beams (17 per side) and a massive keel hewn from one piece of timber still extant. Thirty-two shields still bearing traces of yellow/blue pigment were affixed to the sides of the vessel.

There were definite indications that this was a burial ship—a site for the entombment of a well-known personage. The interior deck was littered with animal remains—primarily bones of horses and dogs. Further investigation revealed that the inner compartment, the actual burial chamber, had previously been ransacked, and any objects of monetary value removed. (The sole exception to this was a small golden goblet, approximately 15 centimeters in height, inlaid with semiprecious stones.) The contents that did remain included metal buttons, buckles, and strap terminals; fragments of a wooden bedstead and chair; and bits of textile with golden and silken thread interwoven in them. The chamber also contained the bones of a male of approximately 50 years of age, who was in poor health at the time of his death; the individual had obviously suffered from some sort of paralysis which had led to abnormal bone structure.

Excavation is still in progress, and I plan to continue other excavations in the area as well, should sufficient funding be available. A complete report of my findings will be presented at our September meeting.

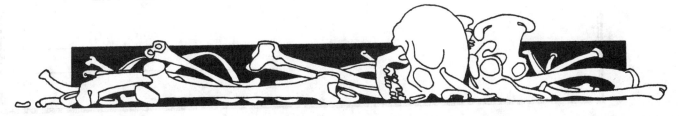

Name _____

Uncovering Purpose

Mr. Deagen is now in need of your help. Draft a letter of appeal to the members of the Society of Amateur Archaeologists. Your purpose is to convince them to provide funds for additional excavations. Remember, your audience consists of laymen—persons without actual training in archaeology—who are enthralled with the idea of "uncovering" valuable historical objects.

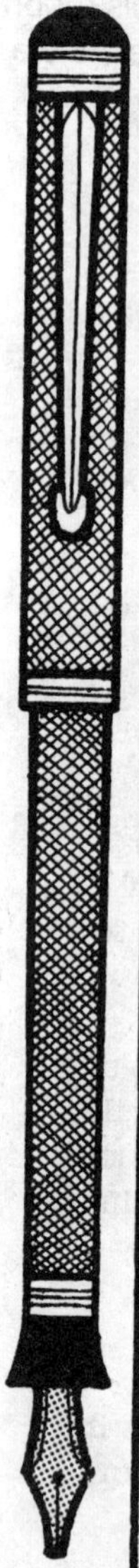

From the desk of G. Deagen

Dear Archaeology Buffs,
    I'm certain that you will be as excited as I was to learn of an important new archaeological find.

Name _____

Make It to the Top

The **plot** is the sequence of events in a story. **Sequencing** means putting the events in chronological order—the order in which they actually occurred.

In 1953, when Edmund Hillary and Tenzing Norgay reached the summit of Mount Everest, they had succeeded where innumerable others before them had failed. Many ascents of the world's highest mountain peak had been attempted, the most tragic in 1924 when Leigh Mallory and Andrew Irving disappeared after being seen only eight hundred feet below the summit. It was only through careful planning and training that the Hillary-Norgay team was able to succeed.

The events on page 20 chronicle Hillary and Norgay's historic climb, but they are out of order. To make it to the top, arrange these events in the order in which they actually occurred by writing each sentence number on the appropriate flag.

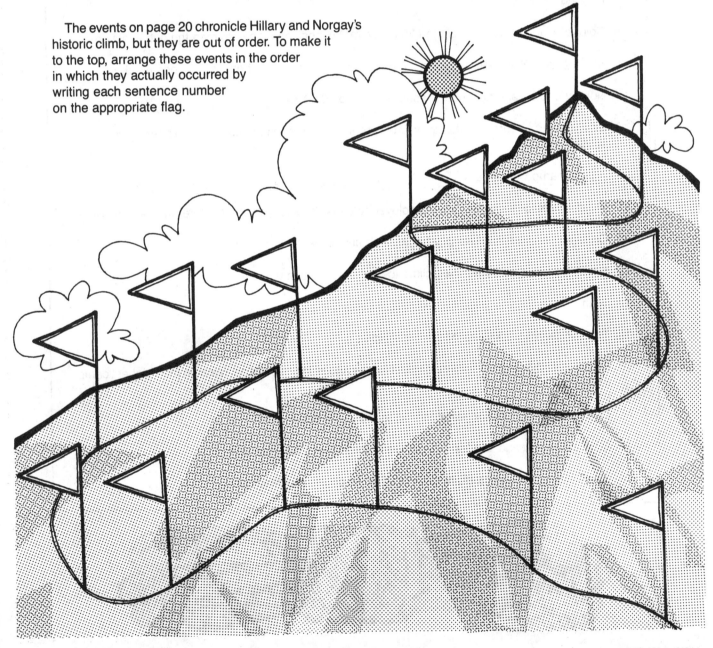

Name _____

Make It to the Top
(continued)

1. All preparations for the actual assault on the peak were finally completed.

2. The equipment and supplies that would be needed were gathered at the base camp.

3. On May 29 at 11:30 A.M., they reached the summit of Mount Everest.

4. The two teams learned to work together, carrying light loads and practicing with the oxygen tanks they would need.

5. Colonel Slade, the leader of the Mount Everest expedition, began to plan the actual ascent.

6. Norgay and Hillary had to stay in the high camp for three days because of poor weather.

7. Norgay and Hillary reached the south summit by 9:00 A.M.

8. Dr. Evans and Bourdillon attempted the ascent, but they had to return to camp after reaching the south summit.

9. A base camp was set up.

10. Hundreds of local sherpas were employed to carry the supplies and to store and care for them.

11. On May 29, Hillary and Norgay began their final ascent.

12. Hillary and Norgay began their climb toward the high camp.

13. Teams became smaller as the expedition neared the top.

14. The two teams worked hard to get in shape.

15. On May 28, the weather finally cleared; Norgay and Hillary moved on, pitching their highest camp in the ice.

16. Dr. Evans and Bourdillon were chosen to make the first attempt.

17. Edmund Hillary and Tenzing Norgay were chosen as a backup team.

18. Small teams began establishing camps higher on the mountain face.

Name _____

CPR—A Real Lifesaver

CPR, the acronym for cardiopulmonary resuscitation, is a life-saving technique that is being taught throughout the United States. It is used to revive persons whose hearts have stopped beating, most commonly as the result of a heart attack.

The essay below describes the CPR technique. Read it carefully, then turn to page 22.

Before you begin CPR, check to be sure that the victim is not breathing and that there is no heartbeat. This technique should *not* be used if there is any pulse, however weak!

Begin by placing the victim flat on his or her back on the ground or floor. Kneel beside the victim's head. Carefully clear the victim's mouth of any foreign matter. Now, gently lift the victim's neck with one hand as you push down on the forehead with the palm of your other hand. Use the fingers of the hand resting on the forehead to pinch the nostrils together. Then, take a deep breath, seal your lips tightly over the victim's mouth, and exhale. Release your mouth, take another deep breath, and repeat the procedure four times, each time releasing your mouth.

At this point, take an eight-second pulse check. If the heart is now beating, continue the breathing technique (at the rate of twelve breaths per minute) until the victim regains consciousness.

If the heart is not beating, place the index and middle fingers of one hand on the tip of the breastbone in the center of the chest. Place the heel of your other hand directly over the wrist of the hand resting on the breastbone. Lean directly over the victim and straighten your arms. This will push the breastbone against the heart. Now relax, releasing the pressure, but leaving your hands on the chest. Repeat this pressure-relaxation combination fifteen times, at the rate of approximately eighty per minute. Now, breathe two times into the person's mouth, following the technique used at the start. Then repeat the pressure-relaxation procedure.

Continue the combined procedure of breaths and pressure-relaxation, giving two breaths after every fifteen chest compressions, until you feel a pulse. When you detect a pulse, discontinue the pressure-relaxation technique but continue artificial respiration until the victim regains consciousness or help arrives.

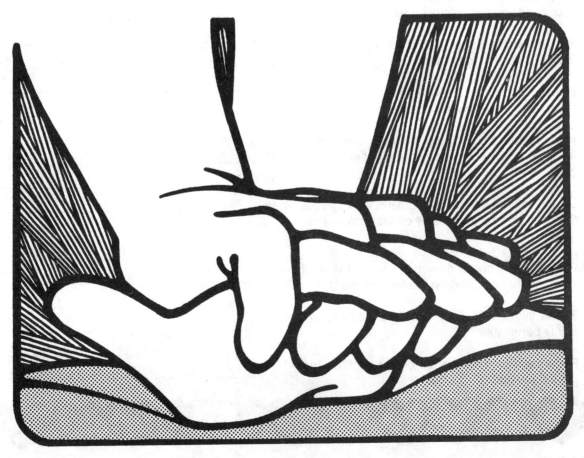

Name _____

CPR—A Real Lifesaver
(continued)

The steps followed in administering CPR to a cardiac arrest victim are listed below, but they are out of order. Indicate the correct order for these steps by writing a step letter on each numbered line. To make your list complete, you'll need to insert the three steps that have been carelessly omitted from the list.

A. Release the mouth, take another deep breath, and repeat this procedure four times.

B. Lean directly over the victim and straighten your arms, pushing the victim's breastbone against the heart.

C. Take an eight-second pulse check.

D. Pinch the victim's nostrils together.

E. Kneel beside the victim's head.

F. Continue this procedure until you feel a pulse.

G. Clear the victim's mouth of any foreign matter.

H. Relax your arms and release the pressure, leaving your hands on the victim's chest.

I. Take a deep breath, seal your lips tightly over the victim's mouth, and exhale.

J. Breathe twice into the victim's mouth and then repeat the pressure-relaxation technique.

K. If you find no pulse, place the index and middle fingers of one hand on the tip of the victim's breastbone.

L. Lift the victim's neck with one hand while resting the palm of your other hand on the victim's forehead.

M. Place the heel of your other hand over the wrist of the hand that is resting on the breastbone.

N. Repeat this combination fifteen times, at the rate of eighty per minute.

O. Place the victim flat on his or her back on the ground or floor.

1. _____
_____
_____
2. _____
3. _____
4. _____
5. _____
6. _____
7. _____
8. _____
9. _____
10. _____
_____
11. _____
12. _____
13. _____
14. _____
15. _____
16. _____
17. _____
18. _____
_____
_____
_____
_____
_____
_____

Diary of a Gold Miner

To write the text for any paragraph, you need a topic, or **main idea**, and you need the details to support that idea. These **supporting details** clarify your meaning or idea and complete the word picture you are trying to create.

Read these entries from a gold miner's diary. Then turn to page 24.

July 1849

Arrived at diggin's today. I'm downstream from a huge waterfall that slides hundreds of feet down the side of a canyon. Took some doin' to get here. Had to climb down the sides of a steep cliff to reach the canyon floor where the stream runs. Tried a little panning today, using my washbowl. My rheumatism's giving me fits because of the cold, icy water.

August 15, 18—

My back is plumb wore out, but I figger I'm lucky. Others around me have sores, swollen hands and feet, and dysentery. Some of them never worked with their hands before. It's hard work, but farm work was just as hard, and you didn't have the chance to make it big. I'll never get used to this water, though!

Some of the fellas have tried "coyote hole" mining where you dig a shaft and work in pairs. Seems too dangerous to me. Only yesterday, Eb Smith was badly hurt when the sides of a shaft caved in. I'll stick to panning.

September 3, 18—

Decided to move to a new claim today. After more than a month, I had less than $100 worth of gold. It hardly seems worth it. This area should be better, though. I've staked it out with four pegs, so it's mine. Luckily, no one got here before me. I've thought about taking a partner—but I guess not. When people get desperate, they cheat anyone, even a partner or a friend. There's no law around here. You have to count on a miners' jury. The whole thing seems like a lot more trouble than it's worth. I do get lonely, though—and two of us could do a lot more pannin'.

September 20

Went into town today for supplies. No eggs for me at $3 apiece—nor flour at $800 a barrel. I'll make do. My $100 is long gone, and I'm in debt. This town doesn't help my spirits none, either. It's the Sabbath, but you'd never know it. No church, and lots of men swearin', gamblin', and fightin'. I'm glad I didn't bring the wife with me.

October 12, 18—

My third claim. This time I'm reworking one some other miner has left. Maybe I'll get lucky. If not, I'm pulling out—though I don't know how I'll get back to Illinois without money. The weather's getting colder—this time I've got to hit it big.

October 21, 18—

Gold! I did it—almost $1000—enough to pay my debts and go home. I've had it! I'm leaving this cold, godforsaken place.

Name _____

Strike It Rich

Sift through the diary entries on page 23. Look for supporting details about the topics listed on these five gold nuggets. As you find details, write them on the appropriate nuggets. When you have filled all of the nuggets, you'll have struck it rich.

Mining Techniques

1. _____
_____
2. _____
_____
_____

Gold Mining Towns

1. _____
2. _____
3. _____

Hardships

1. _____
2. _____
3. _____
4. _____

Law

1. _____
_____
2. _____
_____
3. _____

Miners

1. _____
2. _____
3. _____
4. _____
5. _____

Choose one of these five topics. Use the details you've found to write a paragraph about this topic on a separate sheet of paper.

Name _____

Get the Picture?

The **effect** is what happened as a result of something; the **cause** is the reason for what happened.

Example: He enjoyed challenging nature, so he took up mountain climbing.

What happened?   He took up mountain climbing.

For what reason?   He enjoyed challenging nature.

For each picture below, write three sets of cause-and-effect statements. The first statement for Picture A has been written for you.

Picture A

Causes

1. *Because the gold ran out,* _____

2. _____

3. _____

Effects

1. *the town became a ghost town.* _____

2. _____

3. _____

Picture B

Causes

1. _____

2. _____

3. _____

Effects

1. _____

2. _____

3. _____

Chain of Events

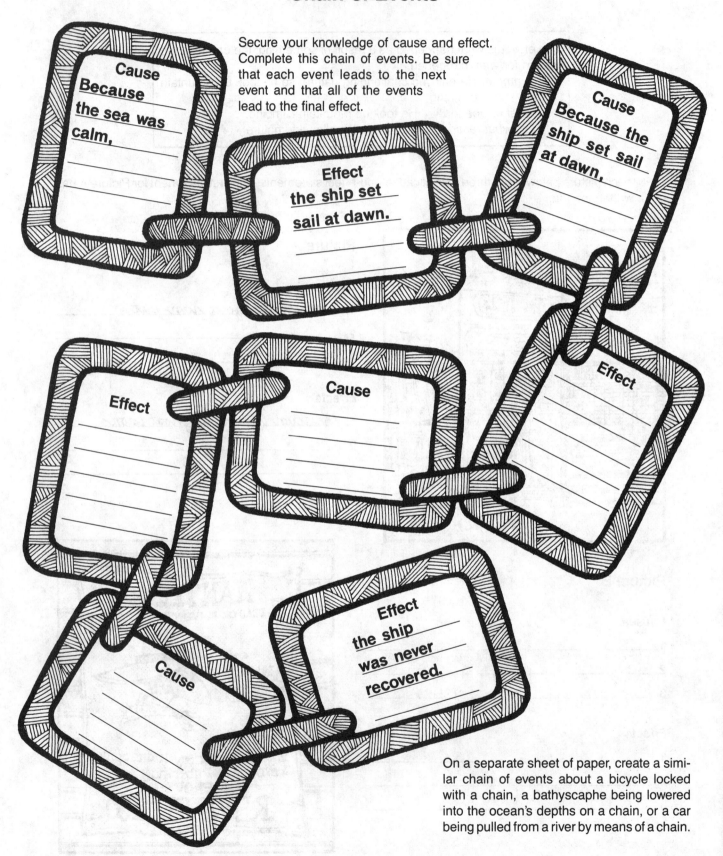

Secure your knowledge of cause and effect. Complete this chain of events. Be sure that each event leads to the next event and that all of the events lead to the final effect.

Cause
Because the sea was calm,

Effect
the ship set sail at dawn.

Cause
Because the ship set sail at dawn,

Effect

Effect

Cause

Cause

Effect
the ship was never recovered.

On a separate sheet of paper, create a similar chain of events about a bicycle locked with a chain, a bathyscaphe being lowered into the ocean's depths on a chain, or a car being pulled from a river by means of a chain.

Name _____

Keys to Conclusions

Drawing conclusions means reaching a decision or making a judgment based on a body of evidence or a group of facts.

Careful reading and observation will enable you to detect certain facts about the keys pictured below. On the basis of these facts, what conclusions can you draw about each key? Record your conclusions on the lines provided.

1. This key was found next to seat 3F after the passengers deplaned from Flight 307 at Los Angeles International Airport.

a. The key would probably open a _____ _____ .

b. It might belong to a _____ _____ .

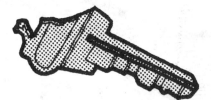

2. This key was found near a railroad track.

a. What is wrong with it? _____ _____

b. What probably happened to it? _____ _____

3. This key belongs to a teen-age girl.

a. What might it unlock? _____ _____

b. What would it be too small to unlock? _____ _____

4. These two keys open the front doors of different houses. What two conclusions can you draw on the basis of these keys?

a. _____ _____ _____

b. _____ _____ _____

Bills, Bills, Bills

Pondering the fate of her son, Cleveland, Amanda Smythers thumbed through the growing stack of bills on her desk. What in the world was the boy up to? Obviously he had decided that college life was not for him. Nevertheless, a postcard or a telephone call did not seem to be too much to expect, especially when he was so freely charging his expenses to her! Spreading the bills in front of her, Amanda resolved to track Cleve down.

The bills Amanda Smythers received are reproduced on page 29. Use them to answer the questions below.

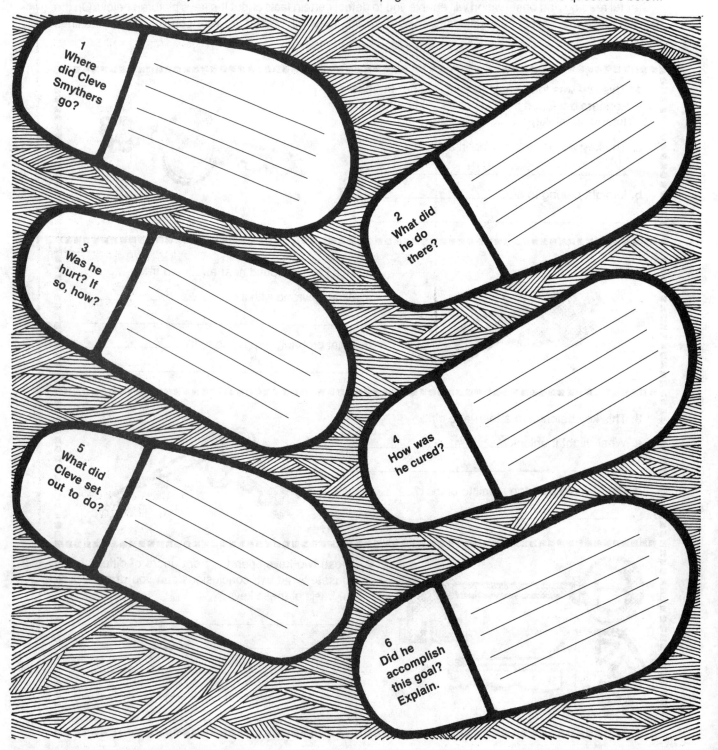

1 Where did Cleve Smythers go?

2 What did he do there?

3 Was he hurt? If so, how?

4 How was he cured?

5 What did Cleve set out to do?

6 Did he accomplish this goal? Explain.

Bills, Bills, Bills
(continued)

ACME SPORTS
Valleyfield, N.H.

Date _9/18/83_

☐ Cash   ☐ Check

☒ Charge To:
Amanda Smythers
Greenwich,
Connecticut

1 sleeping bag	$ 57.30
1 pup tent	135.00
1 camp stove	47.00
50-foot rope	17.50
Total	$ 256.80

CARR-GO OIL CO.
Houston, Texas

J&J Service Station
1 Main Street
Valleyfield, N.H.
Signature _Cleve Smythers_

AMANDA SMYTHERS
Date _9/21_

License No. _F-3742-CT_
Quantity _16.2 gallons_
Price _$1.25_
Charge _$20.25_

ANYBANK CARD
Amanda Smythers

Campy's Campsite
Valleyfield, N.H.

Lodging, 9/18-9/30 .... $84.00

Signature _Cleve Smythers_

ANYBANK CARD
Amanda Smythers

Valleyfield Climbing Guides
Valleyfield, N.H.

Rock climbing instruction, 9/30 .... $45.00

Signature _Cleve Smythers_

Mountain Rescue
Ambulance Service, Inc.

Transportation to Valleyfield
Community Hospital, 10/5 .....
.... $50.00

CARR-GO OIL CO.
Houston, Texas

J&J Service Station
1 Main Street
Valleyfield, N.H.
Signature _Cleve Smythers_

AMANDA SMYTHERS
Date _10/2_

License No. _F-3742-CT_
Quantity _18.8 gallons_
Price _$1.25_
Charge _$23.50_

ANYBANK CARD
Amanda Smythers

Valleyfield Driving Tour
Valleyfield, N.H.

Drive to the top for a view, 11/15 .... $6.00

Signature _Cleve Smythers_

James Meikle, M.D.
ORTHOPEDIC SURGERY
1717 Northrup Way
Valleyfield, N.H.

Set fractured ankle and insert
pin, 10/5 .... $357.00

VALLEYFIELD
COMMUNITY HOSPITAL

10/5-10/9
Emergency room ..	$75.00
Operating room ...	385.00
Plaster of paris	7.85
Room, 5 days at $120 per day	600.00
Total	$1067.85

Soda & Subs
Sandwich
Shop
Date: _Oct. 15_

1 pizza	$7.50
2 colas	1.00
	$8.50

Tom's Surgical Supply
13 Maple Street
Valleyfield, N.H.

1 pair of crutches
10/9 .... $44.00

Ralph Peters
Licensed Physical Therapist

Date: 11/12

Therapy, 2 sessions $85.00

Name _____

Fathom This

The invention pictured here was designed by the world-famous inventor, Jeannie Yuss. Fathom what it is by drawing the correct conclusions. Then answer these questions.

1. What is it? _____

_____

2. Where would it be used? _____

_____

3. Why would it be used? _____

_____

_____

4. How does it work? _____

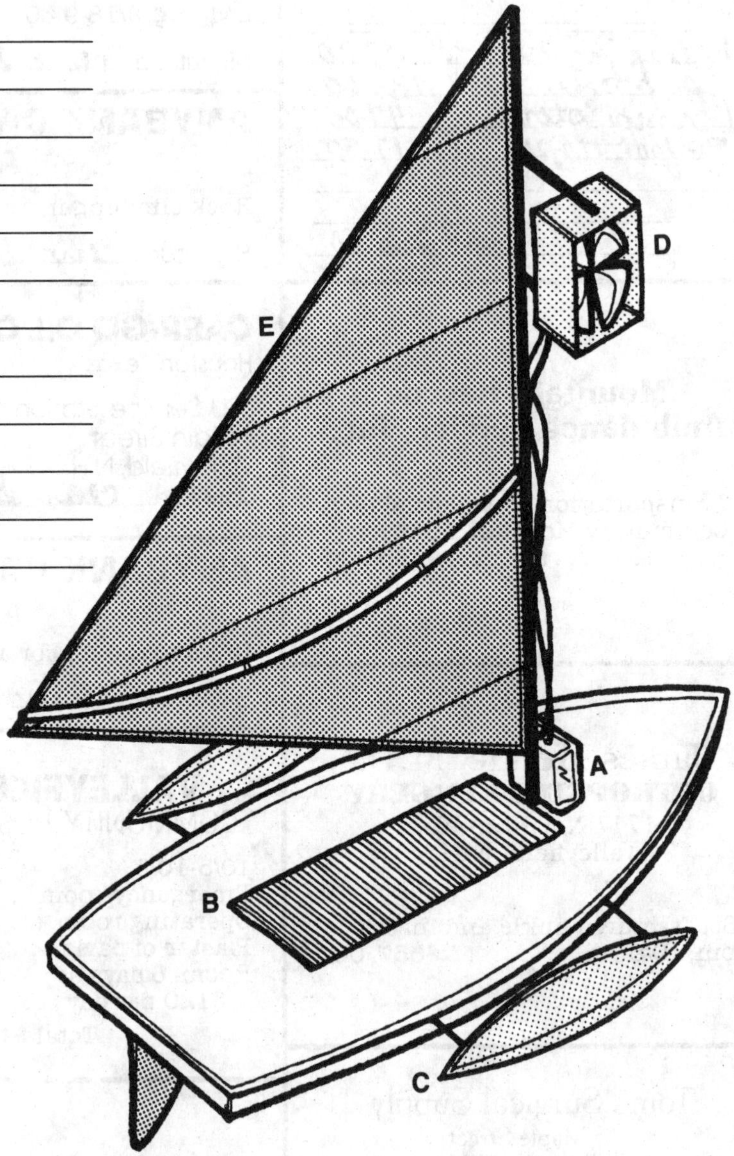

_____

_____

_____

_____

_____

_____

_____

Create an invention of your own. On a separate piece of paper, draw a diagram of your invention. Letter, but do *not* label, all of the important parts. Give your diagram to a friend. Ask the friend to fathom what you have invented by drawing conclusions.

Name _____

A Majestic Decision

> An **inference** is an educated guess based on facts or premises. In the inference process, reasoning is used to come up with a single judgment based on the available evidence.

Charles Intrepid sat in troubled thought at the foot of Mount Majestic. Four exhausted men huddled around the campfire near him, awaiting his decision about the ascent the next day. Night was falling, and they could feel the temperature dropping. Behind them, the north face of the mountain shone, the last rays of the sun reflected off the sheer ice covering it.

That ice was only one of the problems facing Intrepid. The southern face, previously attempted by an old friend, Justin Emory, lay miles away; and it was clear that their supplies were not sufficient for both the trek and the climb. The eastern face was certainly accessible; but it was crisscrossed with ice streams, and the glacier that fed them was cut through with dangerous crevasses.

The responsibility for four other lives weighed heavily on Intrepid. He had to be sure!

That left only the western face, its upper half perpetually enshrouded in mist. Villagers who knew the area well had told Intrepid of easily visible hand and footholds near the base, but the mist precluded any safe assumption that this face held the necessary outcroppings and ledges to establish way camps.

With a sigh, Intrepid roused himself and turned to the shivering men. "Well," he said, "I've made my decision."

1. What did Intrepid decide? _____
_____

2. Why did he make that decision? _____
_____
_____
_____

3. What is the relationship between Intrepid and the four other men? _____
_____

4. Has this group undertaken a major expedition before? _____

5. On what facts is this inference based? _____
_____
_____
_____
_____
_____

6. Is their ascent sponsored by someone? _____

_____

7. What makes you think so? _____

_____
_____
_____

8. Is the mountain close to their homes? _____

9. What information in the text led you to make this inference? _____

_____
_____
_____

Name _____

What's in a Name?

Maps of the Old West are filled with unusual names—names that tell you something about how a place looked or what happened there. What can you infer about each of the places named below?

Angels Camp	Fair Play	Lousy Ravine
Bogus Thunder	Git up and Git	Murderers' Bar
Bonanza	Goldcreek	Poker Flats
Bumblebee	Gunpowder Ridge	Poverty Hill
Carbon Timber Town	Jackrabbit	Rough and Ready
Clip Mine	Lonerock	Snake River
Death Valley	Lookout Hill	World Beater Mine
Dogtown	Lost Oasis	You Bet

Choose one of these places. On a separate sheet of paper, write a fictional account to explain how it received its name. Let your imagination git up and git!

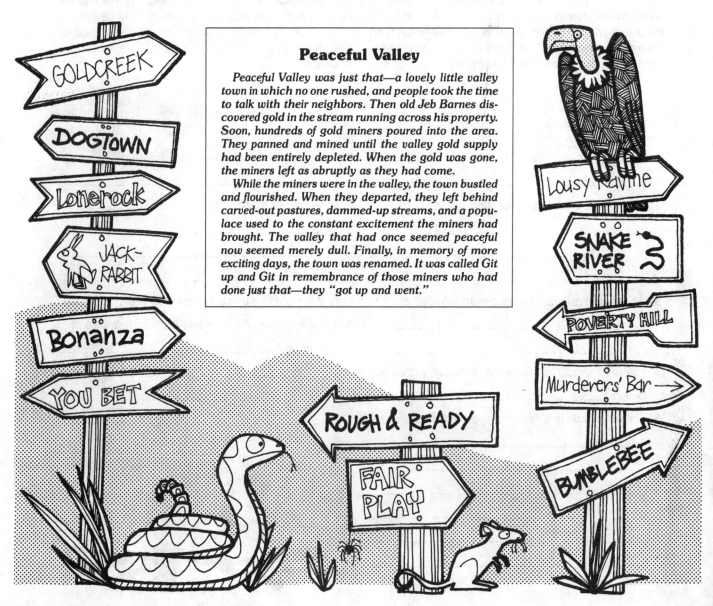

Peaceful Valley

Peaceful Valley was just that—a lovely little valley town in which no one rushed, and people took the time to talk with their neighbors. Then old Jeb Barnes discovered gold in the stream running across his property. Soon, hundreds of gold miners poured into the area. They panned and mined until the valley gold supply had been entirely depleted. When the gold was gone, the miners left as abruptly as they had come.

While the miners were in the valley, the town bustled and flourished. When they departed, they left behind carved-out pastures, dammed-up streams, and a populace used to the constant excitement the miners had brought. The valley that had once seemed peaceful now seemed merely dull. Finally, in memory of more exciting days, the town was renamed. It was called Git up and Git in remembrance of those miners who had done just that—they "got up and went."

Name _____

To the Point

> **Point of view** is the voice the author uses to tell the story. It may be **first person**, in which the author is a character in the story and tells it from his or her point of view.
>
> > *Example:* I've never been as frightened as I was last Saturday afternoon. It was my first parachute jump, and when I pulled the cord, nothing happened.
>
> It may be **third person objective**, in which the author is not a character in the story and is able to report actions and describe events but is not able to tell what the characters are thinking. This point of view is used most often in newspaper stories.
>
> > *Example:* On her first jump last Saturday, Mary's parachute didn't open right away.
>
> It may be **third person omniscient**, in which the author is not a character in the story but is able to look into the characters' minds and report what they are thinking.
>
> > *Example:* Mary panicked when her parachute failed to open immediately.

For each sentence below, identify the point of view that is being used. Write it on the line.

1. "No one can tell me what to do!" shrieked Lucy to her reflection in the mirror.

_____

2. Hector thought of his wife, Maria, as he once again pressed his foot to the brake pedal.

_____

3. John was an avid sportsman.

_____

4. Joanne grimaced as she checked the dial on her air tank.

_____

5. The captain knew that he must not show his fear as he steered his men into enemy waters.

_____

On the lines below, write three sentences for which the point of view is first person.

6. _____

7. _____

8. _____

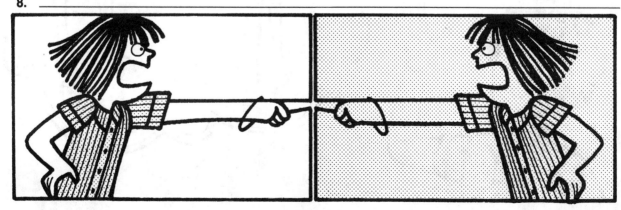

Point-of-View Parade

> Drum up some interest in point of view. In this activity, students get in step by sharing their own real-life adventures.

Instructions

During Class

1. List the three points of view on the board. Discuss each one and give some examples.
2. Divide the class into three teams: First Person, Third Person Objective, and Third Person Omniscient.
3. Ask each member of the First Person team to relate an incident that happened to him or her and to include something he or she *thought* while the incident was occurring.
4. Ask a member of the Third Person Objective team to retell the incident from that viewpoint.
5. Finally, ask a member of the Third Person Omniscient team to retell the incident as one who is able to look into the characters' minds and to know what each one of them is thinking.
6. Continue in this way until every member of the class has had an opportunity to participate.

Follow-up

Have class members complete the To the Point skill sheet on page 33, or ask each one of them to select a real-life incident and describe it from each of the three points of view.

Name _____

Conflict Crossover

> The **protagonist** is the leading character or hero of a story. The **antagonist** is an opponent, the adversary of the protagonist.

Choose the protagonist from one story you have read and the antagonist from another story. Pit them against each other in a totally new adventure tale of your own creation.

Characters

_____, the protagonist

from the story _____

_____, the antagonist

from the story _____

Setting

☐ a catamaran   ☐ a jungle   ☐ outer space

☐ a hot-air balloon   ☐ New York City   ☐ under the sea

☐ other (specify): _____

Title   _____

Story

_____

_____

_____

_____

_____

_____

_____

_____

_____

_____

Use an additional sheet of paper if you need it. When you have finished writing, answer this question: How would your story have been different if *you* had been the protagonist?

Picture Perfect Personalities

There are five ways in which you can tell what a character is like. Consider, for example, Wild Bill Hickok.

1. What the character says:
   Example: "I was a constable, teamster, and stagecoach driver before I came to Abilene."
2. What the character does:
   Example: Wild Bill liked to spend time gambling at the Alamo Saloon.
3. What other characters say about the character:
   Example: "Wild Bill and I had a great time riding, shooting, and gambling together," said Calamity Jane.
4. How other characters act toward the character:
   Example: When Wild Bill and Calamity Jane rode into Deadwood together, people cheered.
5. What the author says about the character:
   Example: At one time, Wild Bill Hickok was a scout for Custer.

Below is a list of some of the best-known monikers from the Old West. Choose one of these nicknames, do some library research on it, and then complete the pictures on page 37.

Bat Masterson	Buffalo Bill Cody	Kid Curry
Big Casino	Cattle Annie	Little Britches
Big Foot Wallace	Cherokee Kid	Long Hair Jim
Billy the Kid	Crazy Horse	Preacher Smith

Name _____

Personality Pictures

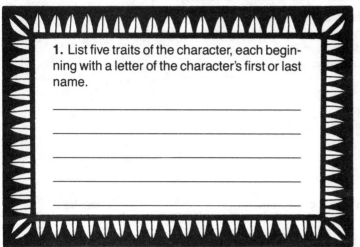

1. List five traits of the character, each beginning with a letter of the character's first or last name.

_____

_____

_____

_____

_____

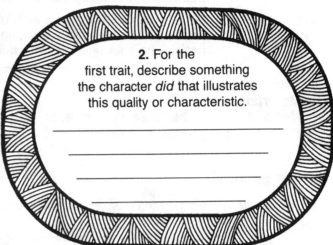

2. For the first trait, describe something the character *did* that illustrates this quality or characteristic.

_____

_____

_____

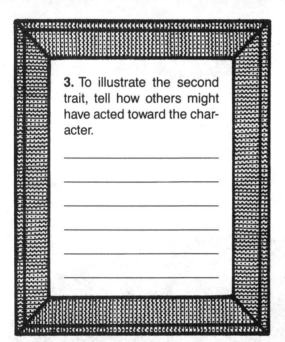

3. To illustrate the second trait, tell how others might have acted toward the character.

_____

_____

_____

_____

_____

_____

4. On the lines below, write what the character might have said that would illustrate the third trait.

_____

_____

_____

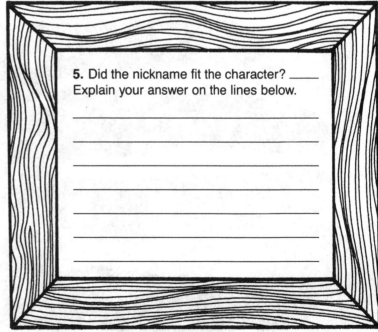

5. Did the nickname fit the character? ____ Explain your answer on the lines below.

_____

_____

_____

_____

_____

_____

_____

6. If you had lived in the Old West, what might your nickname have been?

_____

_____

On a separate sheet of paper, write a paragraph to explain your answer to question 6.

The Creature Feature

Who or what is the huge, four-fingered creature that has invaded your classroom and left black handprints on the walls? Students will learn about characterization as they create this creature.

Materials Needed

black construction paper
masking tape

Instructions

Before Class

1. Using your own hand as a pattern, cut large, four-fingered hands from black construction paper.
2. Tape the hands to the walls of your classroom so that they go from one door or window to another.

During Class

1. Ask the class, *What creature has been in our classroom?*
2. With class members, brainstorm names for the creature.
3. Ask class members to characterize the creature by
   - explaining where it came from and why
   - listing the mannerisms it might have
   - telling why it visited *this* classroom
   - reporting what people *say* when they see it
   - giving examples of what people *do* when the creature is around
   - creating the creature's favorite saying

Follow-up

Create a characterization display by placing the handprints on a bulletin board and adding the students' brainstormed lists to this board.

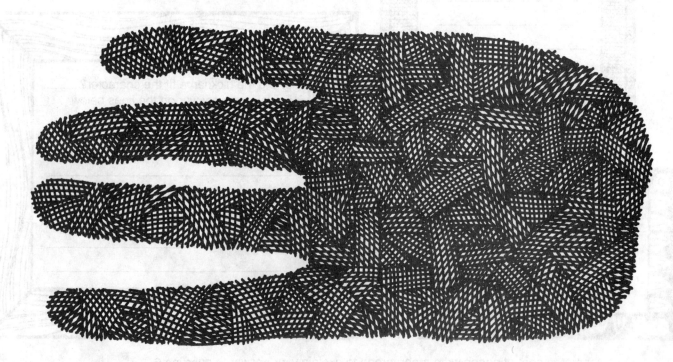

Should You Quote Me?

Read the character sketch below. Then use the information it contains to answer the questions on page 40.

Nancy Woodworth's eyes sparkled as she snugged up the strap of her helmet. She could feel the old exhilaration building as she walked toward the hangar. This mission was going to be a particularly difficult one, because the XT-36 had not yet been tested outside the wind tunnel. The thought was a stimulating one, and her steps quickened. "It's funny," she thought, "the more dangerous the undertaking, the more I enjoy it."

Nancy frowned for a moment, remembering her parents' shocked response when she had told them of her desire to become a test pilot. They didn't understand. Actually, no one seemed to understand, not even Charles, her fiancé. He still seemed so smugly convinced that she would soon be ready to give up her career and settle down in some cute little bungalow somewhere as his wife. She was *certainly* tired of discussing it. She simply couldn't envision any other life-style that would give her the pleasure and satisfaction she derived from being a test pilot. If only Charles would accept her career commitment and stop his endless efforts to persuade her to do something she didn't want to do and to be something she didn't want to be!

She had reached the door to the hangar, where a small crowd of men was waiting. She turned toward them and instantly dismissed her personal concerns from her mind. Her total attention was focused on the important task ahead of her. An anticipatory smile lighted her face.

Should You Quote Me?
(continued)

Read each of the statements about Nancy written below. Compare them with the information about Nancy given in the character sketch on page 39. Then, for each statement, indicate

a. whether it is accurate,

b. which technique of characterization helped you to decide, and

c. the exact words in the sketch that persuaded or convinced you.

1. "Nancy will come to her senses. She's a wonderful girl."

Charles Black

a. _____

b. _____

c. _____
  _____
  _____

2. "Nancy's mother and I just don't feel that Nancy has chosen wisely; she'd be much happier in a job with less tension."

John Woodworth

a. _____

b. _____

c. _____
  _____
  _____

3. "Nancy is a motivated, talented young woman. She thrives on danger. She'll go far in her chosen career."

Jake Williams
Flight Supervisor

a. _____

b. _____

c. _____
  _____
  _____

4. "Nancy really isn't a person you can get close to. I've been her friend for five years, and I still don't feel that I really know her."

Cindy Richards

a. _____

b. _____

c. _____
  _____
  _____
  _____

5. "Nancy has always had the ability to focus on a task to the exclusion of everything else. She was an excellent, conscientious student."

Raymond Jenkins
High School Teacher

a. _____

b. _____

c. _____
  _____
  _____

6. "I prefer to avoid confrontation."

Nancy Woodworth
Test Pilot

a. _____

b. _____

c. _____
  _____
  _____
  _____
  _____
  _____

Name _____

Conflict Connections

A **conflict** is a struggle. Every story includes at least one of the four main types of conflict.

1. **Man vs. Man** involves a direct struggle between two of the characters in the story. Examples are a man and wife who disagree about how their money should be spent; two little boys engaged in a fistfight; a boss who is firing an employee.
2. **Man vs. Nature** involves a struggle between a character and elements of nature that are beyond his control. Examples are a family stranded by a snowstorm; a woman who is unable to function because of illness; a man stalked by a wild animal in the forest.
3. **Man vs. Society** involves the struggle between a character and the rules or laws that govern the society in which he lives. Examples are a woman who runs a red light; a child who plays hooky; a burglar who breaks into a house.
4. **Man vs. Himself** involves the struggle between the character and his conscience. Examples are a woman who is tempted to steal money from her employer; a child who cannot decide whether or not to lie to his mother about his reason for arriving home late; a man who would like to quit his job.

Some of the situations described below involve conflicts, and some do not. Draw a line from each conflict situation to the type of conflict it involves. Then, on the lines at the bottom of the page, write the numbers of the two situations that do *not* involve conflicts and add conflicts to them.

1. John and his father play chess.
2. Earlene attempts to swim the English Channel.
3. Hector goes to work.
4. Hudson Smith, the famous race car driver, exceeds the highway speed limit.

Man vs. Man
Man vs. Nature
Man vs. Society
Man vs. Himself

5. Peter and Kyle watch television.
6. Lizzie tries to decide whether to go hang gliding or stay home and study for a test.
7. Caroline is trapped by a hurricane.

____ _____

_____

____ _____

_____

Name _____

Conflict Campout

A story without a conflict is like a tent without a camper—empty! In fact, most stories contain more than one conflict. Read this passage. Then, on the lines below, introduce a conflict within the same setting.

Rob hummed along as he stared across the dying fire at Jimmy and Chris and reviewed in his mind the exhilarating day just ending. Luckily, they had arrived at Wehahadin early enough to set up camp, pitch their tents, and still have time left for exploration. His fears that the spot would not live up to his memories of it had been unfounded. If anything, the colors were brighter; the smells, sweeter; and the air, crisper, than he had remembered. "This is the place for me," he thought.

As always, the boys had made a game of readying the tents. Rob had not been bothered when Jimmy and Chris won the race. After all, they were younger than he, and far more competitive. At any rate, he had finished soon enough to accompany them to Bear Paw Falls, named for the black bears that were known to drink there.

The boys had paid little attention to the sounds of the woods as they approached the falls. They had been startled by a dark shape looming above them. Suddenly, . . .

_____

_____

_____

_____

_____

_____

_____

_____

_____

_____

_____

Name _____

Scale the Heights

> The **climax** of a story is the turning point, the moment at which the conflict is resolved.

In most plots, **characters** in a particular **setting** become involved in a **conflict**. This conflict leads to **rising action**, in which they try to resolve the conflict. Their efforts result in a **climax**, in which the conflict is resolved. Resolution of the conflict is followed by **falling action**, during which related minor problems are solved, and then by the **ending**. Plots of this type can be diagramed as shown below.

Climax or Turning Point
They were rescued by the captain of a passing motorboat.

Conflict: Man vs. Nature
A huge storm caused their tour boat to overturn.

Falling Action
They returned to their hotel and changed to dry clothes.

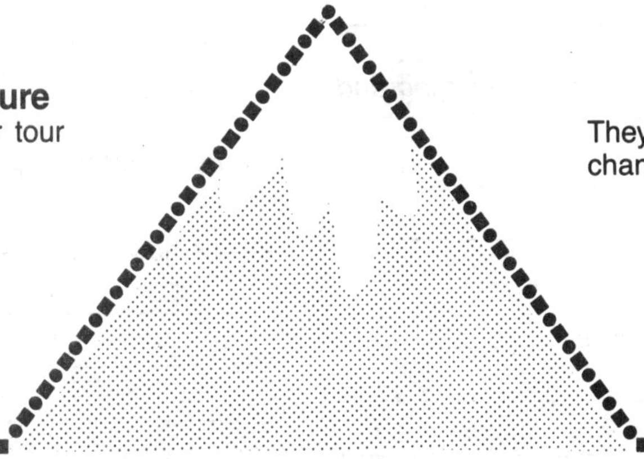

Setting and Characters
John and Debby went to Niagara Falls for a vacation.

Ending
The tour boat company sent them a gift certificate for a free dinner.

Look at the example above. Then scale the heights for a story you have read by filling in the diagram below.

Climax or Turning Point
_____
_____
_____

Conflict
_____
_____
_____

Falling Action
_____
_____
_____

Setting and Characters
_____
_____
_____

Ending
_____
_____
_____

Name _____

Figure It Out

> **Figurative language** is any language that is used creatively and imaginatively to evoke vivid images and fresh insights.

These five sentences contain figurative language. Read the sentences. Then, for each one, indicate
a. what *two things* are being compared and
b. what the *literal meaning* is.

1. *The mountain towered over him.*

a. The mountain is being compared to a _____
_____.

b. This means that the mountain is _____
_____.

2. *The big wave climbed toward him, twisting and turning like a serpent in its fury.*

a. The _____

and a/an _____

are being compared.

b. This means that the wave was _____
_____
_____.

3. *The wind bit into him as he traversed the treacherous slope.*

a. To what is the wind being compared? _____
_____

b. _____
_____
_____
_____

4. *Like a vise, his hand grasped the rope.*

a. _____
_____
_____

b. _____
_____
_____

c. Why is this an effective comparison?
_____
_____

5. *The flower wept petals, bidding farewell to summer.*

a. The flower's petals are being compared to
_____.

b. _____
_____
_____

c. What feeling does this image convey? _____
_____
_____

Name _____

Figure Eight

The author of this story did not realize that comparisons used to evoke vivid images must be appropriate ones. Help her! Find the eight figures of speech that are not at all suited to the story, underline them, and then write more appropriate alternatives on the lines provided below the story.

The night of the Women's World Figure Skating Championship had arrived. In the dressing room, Christine paced like a wounded guinea pig as she waited for her name to be called. She'd done well in the school figures and had every reason to expect that she would win the fast-footed world title this year. She'd been disappointed—a soggy potato chip—when she'd placed second to Irina Blovoda in last year's Olympics. She and Irina got along as well as peas in a pod off the ice, but engaged in a constant battle in their skating lives. They followed each other from one international competition to another like dehydrated aardvarks.

There it was, her name blaring like a bassoon from the public address system. She hurried toward the rink. The noise of the crowd, a chorus of one thousand screeching violins, started her adrenalin flowing. By the time she reached center ice, she was ready to perform the routine she had practiced more than two thousand times. As the spotlight pulverized her and the familiar strains of a Strauss waltz filled the arena, Chris knew that this was going to be her best night ever, that she was going to win!

1. _____

2. _____

3. _____

4. _____

5. _____

6. _____

7. _____

8. _____

Name _____

Back in a Flash

A **flashback** is an interruption in a story to permit the author to relate an event from the past.

Lieutenant Melinda Brier of the United States Military Space Squad hurriedly grabbed the pencil that floated in front of her. As Mark Walworth, the new commander of the USS *Starstop*, leaned anxiously over her shoulder, she pointed to the diagram on the screen to their left. They were practically surrounded by Praknian spaceships. Throwing the pencil away in disgust, Melinda sank back dejectedly in her seat. Who would have thought it would all end like this?

Melinda closed her eyes and thought back to her days in college when she had dreamed of nothing more than becoming an electrical engineer. That had been in 1983, when there were few openings for women in the United States space program. She had studied hard and graduated fourth in her class from Hanby University. A job with Champlain Electrical Products followed, but she had soon found herself bored with the routine work. Through a quirk of fate, she had met Dave Roberts, who secured a position for her with the Delta Space Investigation Team. Thus it was that she had been in the right place at the right time when the Military Space Squad sought a replacement for a navigator. And up until this moment, Melinda had loved her job.

Snapping out of her reverie, Melinda turned back to the computer screen, determined to steer the fleet out of danger.

On the lines below, write another flashback, this one involving Commander Walworth.

_____

_____

_____

_____

_____

_____

_____

_____

_____

_____

_____

MILITARY SPACE SQUAD

Turn Back the Clock

> The element of chance will inspire even the most reluctant writer to participate in this lesson on flashback.

Materials Needed

chalkboard
chalk
one story with many events
an index card or small piece of paper for each student in the class
a box, can, fishbowl, hat, or other similar widemouthed container

Instructions

Before Class   Select a story with many events.

During Class
1. Have all members of the class read the story you have selected, or read it aloud to them.
2. With the class, brainstorm a list of events from the story.
3. List all of the events in the story in order on the board.
4. At the same time, have a scribe record each event *except the first* on an index card or small piece of paper.
5. Put the cards or pieces of paper into the widemouthed container.
6. Review the definition of flashback, and emphasize the need for a smooth transition between present and past events.
7. Have each student draw a card or piece of paper from the container.
8. Tell students to rewrite the story beginning with the events they have drawn. (In this way, each version of the story will contain a flashback.)

Follow-up   Have students write original adventure stories that include flashbacks.

Name _____

Forecast the Foreshadowing

> **Foreshadowing** is giving an indication or warning of what is to come so that the reader can anticipate the mood or action.

A weather forecaster is often called upon to predict the weather based on signs, or clues. What predictions, or forecasts, can you make based on the foreshadowing clues given in the sentences below? First, underline the specific foreshadowing clue. Then, write what you feel it foreshadows.

1. *You are spelunking in a cave when suddenly your candle goes out.*

_____

_____

2. *You are skydiving when you sense a dark shadow above you.*

_____

_____

3. *You are exploring an abandoned house when you come across some unspoiled milk.*

_____

_____

_____

4. *You awaken in the morning to find that your guide and all of your bearers have hastily fled your jungle encampment, leaving their possessions behind.*

_____

_____

5. *You have battened down the hatches and gone below, when you hear a series of thuds on the deck overhead.*

_____

_____

_____

_____

6. *You return from a secret reconnaissance to find a large box sitting on your doorstep.*

_____

_____

_____

_____

7. *You are searching for firewood far from your wilderness camp when you discover that the falling snow has obliterated your tracks.*

_____

_____

_____

8. *You are setting a fast pace in a marathon when you notice a shoelace beginning to trail.*

_____

_____

_____

_____

9. *You are pitching your tent on a precipice on Mount Cloud when you notice that your companion is nowhere in sight.*

_____

_____

_____

10. *You are paddling a canoe down the Snake River rapids when you suddenly notice a smooth, V-shaped section of water ahead.*

_____

_____

_____

Name _____

Foreshadowing Forecast: Danger Ahead!

You are in the unique position of knowing what disaster will occur next in each of the situations described below. It's your job to provide a foreshadowing clue for the reader. The first one has been done for you.

Situation	Foreshadowing clue	Disaster Ahead
1. You are riding out a fierce storm when…	*you hear a loud snap*	your mast is washed overboard.
2. You are bicycling in France when…	_____ _____	the axle holding your front tire gives way.
3. You are surfing in Hawaii when…	_____ _____	a huge wave crests above you and breaks your board.
4. You are working on a dig in Egypt when…	_____ _____	you discover the entrance to a hidden burial chamber.
5. You are rappelling from a mountain peak when…	_____ _____	one of the pitons holding your rope pulls loose.
6. You are making your escape from an enemy prison camp when…	_____ _____	you encounter a guard dog.
7. You are hiking alone on a warm summer day when…	_____ _____	you find yourself in an abandoned well.
8. You are paddling your kayak downstream when…	_____ _____	you find yourself looking at the bottom of the streambed.
9. When you raise the periscope of your submarine and look out,…	_____ _____	you see two eyes peering in.
10. You are returning from your first solo flight when…	_____ _____	you notice that the landing strip is not in view.

Name _____

Mood Messages

> **Mood** is the feeling an author wishes to create for the reader. Mood may be created by means of setting, situation, and description separately, or by any combination of these three elements.

Each of these paragraphs contains a sentence that does not fit the mood of the paragraph. Can you find the sentence that does not fit?

I. Setting: Like a sea of sparkling diamonds responding to the first bright rays of morning sunlight, the meadow grass danced gently to and fro as the wind whispered by. At the edge of the field, young saplings stood silent guard over the start of the day. The roar of a lion thundered through the nearby woods. Underfoot, wildflowers created a carpet of dappled color.

1. Underline the sentence that does not fit the mood of this paragraph.

2. On the lines below, write a sentence that better suits the mood of the paragraph.

_____

_____

_____

_____

II. Description: Tom was halfway to the top. Once again checking the ropes on which his very life depended, he instinctively dug his spikes in harder in an attempt to grasp the granite wall he was determined to scale. Light, sparkling snowflakes wafted past him. Only last week, Smith Hastings, the renowned rock climber, had fallen near this very spot. Knowing that even a small error in judgment could prove fatal, Tom carefully began to inch his way upward.

1. Underline the sentence that does not fit.

2. On the lines below, write a paragraph into which this sentence could fit.

_____

_____

_____

_____

_____

_____

_____

_____

_____

_____

_____

_____

_____

_____

_____

_____

_____

_____

Name _____

Mood Messages
(continued)

III. Situation: Jane couldn't believe that she had ended up in a situation like this. Only yesterday, she had embarked on a cruise that had been billed as "the single girl's dream." Desperately clutching the life ring she had grabbed as the boat sank, Jane tried to push aside thoughts of the sharks that were known to frequent these waters. Her thoughts drifted happily to the sun and fun she had expected. Suddenly, as the rain pelted down around her, she felt something hard scrape against her leg.

1. What mood do the majority of the sentences in this paragraph work together to create?

_____

_____

2. Circle the words that help to create this mood.

3. Underline the sentence that does not fit the mood of the paragraph.

4. On the lines below, rewrite the sentence so that it does fit with the rest of the paragraph.

_____

_____

_____

_____

Name _____

Focus on the Setting

Setting is the time and place in which an event occurs.

Read these four passages. Then, focus on the setting. For each passage, underline those details that allowed you to determine the setting. On the lines below each passage, indicate
a. the time and
b. the place that has been established.

1. Smooth, streamlined shapes glided past, shimmering with blues and greens, their silent journey punctuated by the stream of bubbles rising from Lucas's tank. After a quick, confident glance at his watch, he continued his descent.

a. _____

b. _____

2. Reginald Raleigh walked cautiously at the head of a line of bearers. In his hands he held a compass and a map. The noonday sun beat down mercilessly on his head; and dense, damp underbrush clung to his legs as he moved past. He was exhausted, and the muted grumbling behind him told him that the others were tired as well.

a. _____

b. _____

3. The silence of the takeoff awed the spectators, who clustered in small, uneasy groups. The white, glistening sphere rose slowly, hovering above them like a giant mushroom. Then, suddenly, it was gone. The crowd dispersed, hoping that this last mission would prove successful.

a. _____

b. _____
_____

4. It was evening. The wind was still, and the silence was absolute. Ian Conway stood quietly on the mountain peak, his mittened hands loosely clasped, his head bowed. In front of him the sun sank slowly, casting mauve and amber shadows on the surrounding peaks. With a quiet sigh, Ian turned and prepared for the descent.

a. _____

b. _____

Picture This!

Owen Stage, the well-known playwright, has just completed a drama based on Gawn Deagen's discovery of the lost burial ship (see page 17). The play focuses on the moment at which Deagan identifies the vessel. Create a stage setting that will allow members of the audience to imagine themselves on an archaeological dig and to visualize the ruins of the ship. Your setting must be consistent with the mood Mr. Stage is trying to establish. Be sure that it conveys Deagen's elation at finding the ship and his subsequent disappointment at discovering that the inner compartment has been ransacked.

Using your sketch as a guide, write a verbal description of the discovery setting as you imagine it. Be sure to include sensory details—the sights, sounds, smells, colors, and textures of an old vessel and an archaeological dig. Use an additional sheet of paper if necessary.

_____

_____

_____

_____

_____

_____

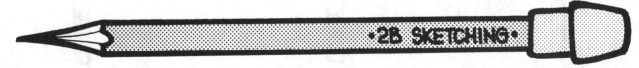

Name _____

Symbol Signs

> A **symbol** is an object, person, place, or event that can be used to stand for, represent, or suggest something else because of traditional association, emotional content, or accidental resemblance. For example, an apple may be used to suggest school because of traditional association. For the same reason, a four-leaf clover symbolizes good luck.

The first annual Careers Convention is scheduled for next week. Representatives of every career imaginable will attend. Sara Synamaker must paint the placards that will show each group where to meet. For physicians, she will probably use the caduceus, their well-known symbol; however, some of the less common occupations have her stumped. Help Sara by creating an appropriate symbol for each of the exciting careers named below.

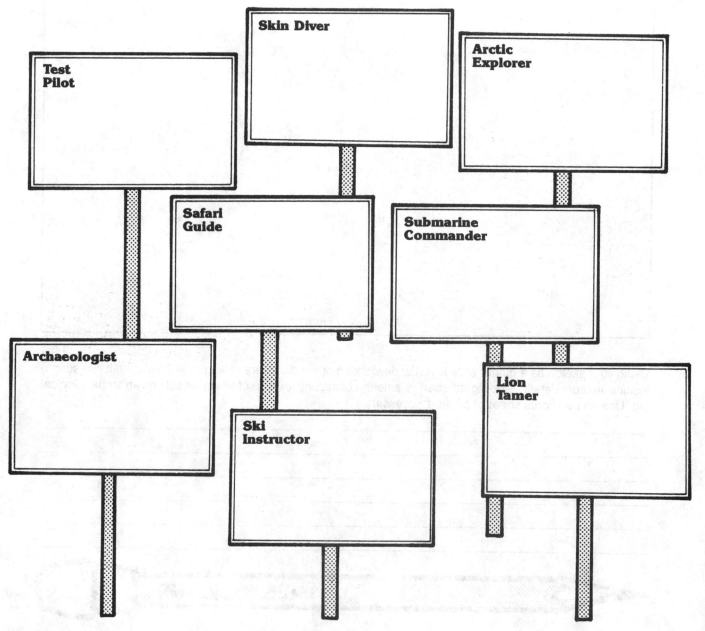

Theme River Raft Race

The **theme** is the subject or topic of discourse or artistic representation. It is an idea about life expressed by an author or artist in a literary or artistic work.

Thea and her friends worked for a week to prepare their raft for the Theme River Raft Race. Saturday, the day of the race, dawned gray and cloudy. Nevertheless, the girls chattered happily as they pushed their raft into the water. After hopping aboard, they anxiously awaited the starting gun. And then, they were off!

Unfortunately, they ran into some obstacles along the way. At each obstacle, create an event to illustrate the given theme. The first one has been done for you.

1. Courage: They hadn't gone one hundred yards when the corner of their raft, *Thea-ma-rig*, caught under the jutting root of a dead tree. Thea immediately jumped into the freezing water to free the craft. Giving little thought to her own safety, she dove under the vessel and tugged on the offending root, allowing the raft to resume its journey.

2. Betrayal

_____
_____
_____
_____
_____
_____
_____
_____
_____
_____

3. Determination

_____
_____
_____
_____
_____
_____
_____
_____
_____

Name _____

Safari Strain

> **Tone** is the style or manner of expression in speaking or writing. It reflects the author's attitude toward the spoken or written material.

The writers of the (1) journal entry, (2) log entry, and (3) personal letter reproduced on this page certainly differ in their attitudes toward the safari they are on. Read their accounts. For each one, underline the words that set the tone. Then, on the appropriately numbered line below, name or describe the tone that these words set.

(1)

10/14
Satisfactory day. Observed four elephant herds—innumerable gazelle and crested cranes. Charged by rhino annoyed by our presence. Irma showed her usual lack of control. Back to lodge at 6:00—bed at 9:00.

G.V.

Silver Safari Tours
Daily Log

(2)

The usual assortment of middle-aged, overweight, and out-of-shape passengers. I'm glad you'll be taking over tomorrow. I'm losing my sense of humor.

Had a small brush with five rhino today. No damage to Rover or passengers—except perhaps for hearing damage caused by Irma Vreenland's screams. (Actually, it was an amazing display; I had no idea a human being could sustain a scream for five solid minutes!) The whole incident was unnecessary—brought on by Mr. Smith's dropping his film cartridge. Rhino were startled and charged, so I made a fast exit. (You'll come to love Mr. Smith; his possessions are scattered all over East Africa.)

Try southeastern corner of the park tomorrow. It looks promising.

John

(3)

Dear Agnes,
What a day! I'm dusty, shaken, and exhausted. This is fun! I tried to tell George that a safari wouldn't be all he had hoped, but would he listen? Anyway, even I didn't know it would be death-defying.
Wait until you hear! This morning we were bouncing and jouncing over the plains when our driver spotted a herd of rhino and moved closer. The rhino seemed fine until Freddie Smith dropped his film cartridge out the window. The next thing I knew, they were charging. I almost died! Our driver finally got the car in gear with a terrific lurch (my neck is still aching), and we took off with the rhino close behind. Eventually, thank heavens, they gave up, and we returned to the lodge.
And to top it off, George is furious with me. He claims my screams deafened him and the others in the Land Rover. Isn't that just like a man—to complain about a little noise in a terrifying situation!
Off to bed. Say hello to little Hubert for me.

Love,
Irma

1. _____

2. _____

3. _____

Name That Tone

Students have the opportunity to use and identify various tones while participating in this speaking activity.

Materials Needed

sentence and tone cards on page 58
scissors
tagboard or construction paper
white glue
laminating plastic or clear Contact paper

Instructions

Before Class

1. Photocopy page 58.
2. Cut apart the sentence and tone cards.
3. To make these cards more durable, glue them to tagboard or construction paper and laminate or cover with clear Contact paper.
4. Put the sentence cards in one pile and the tone cards in another.

During Class

1. Tell class members that **tone** is the style or manner of expression in speaking or writing and reflects the speaker's or writer's attitude toward the spoken or written material. Just as a person's tone of voice can give very different meanings to what is being said, an author's choice of words can influence the overall feeling and interpretation of a passage he or she has written.
2. In turn, each student selects one sentence card and one tone card.
3. The student says the selected sentence in the specified tone.
4. Other members of the class attempt to "name that tone."
5. The first student to identify the tone correctly becomes the next speaker.
6. After each student speaks, return the cards to the piles. Continue playing until each sentence has been voiced in many tones, and each student has had a turn.

Follow-up

Have class members create additional sentence and tone cards to use when playing this game.

Sentence and Tone Cards

It's coming straight toward us.	admiring
What are you up to now?	amazed
What made you decide to do that?	amused
Where did you come from?	angry
How did you get in here?	anxious
You can't do that here.	bored
Where have you been?	confused
Do you know what time it is?	detached
I can't wait.	enthusiastic
Jump.	excited
When will you ever learn?	exhausted
How much longer will it be?	frightened
It's gigantic.	impatient
Where did you learn to do that?	resentful
It's mine.	sarcastic
No one has ever tried that before.	surprised

HOW DID YOU GET IN HERE?

An Undersea Adventure with a Twist

Your students are sure to enjoy the twists and turns in this literary skill review entitled "A Perfect Day?"

1. Photocopy pages 59-66.
2. Cut the episodes apart along the dotted lines.
3. Either duplicate enough copies of each episode so that every member of the class can have one or make a transparency.
4. On the first day, read the Introduction aloud to the class, and discuss the questions that follow.
5. Ask members of the group to decide whether they wish to read Episode A or Episode B.
6. On the next day, read the episode they selected, discuss the questions that follow it, and decide which episode to read on the following day.
7. Continue in this fashion for two more days.

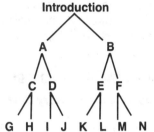

Because the outcome of the story depends on the episodes the class selects (see diagram), this activity can be used several times with the same class—but with different results each time.

A Perfect Day?

Introduction

The surface of the water was ripple free, a blue-green calm that beckoned to him. With an excited smile, Lucas began to put on his gear. A wet suit was followed by flippers, tanks, a mask, and a net bag containing an underwater camera and a notebook. He moved toward the edge of the rail, then paused and, in one smooth motion, removed his spear gun from its deckside holder and fastened it to his belt. Confident that he was finally ready, he threw a float over the side of the boat and then carefully lowered himself, backward, into the water.

As the water closed over his head, he felt a stab of concern. He could almost hear Rick, his instructor, reminding the class how important it was to dive with a partner—or at least with someone on board. But there hadn't been time. He had the use of the boat only today, and reports of the fish off this reef were tantalizing. He was sure he'd get all of the shots he needed; he had all day, and it was only early morning. He'd just have to be especially careful.

1. *What is the **setting** of this story?* _____

2. *Who is the **main character**?* _____

3. *In what activities is he currently engaged?* _____

4. *What type of **conflict** is present in this passage?* _____

5. *At what point does the author **flash back** to an earlier event?* _____

_____

6. *Why?* _____

7. *What words or statements **foreshadow** a change of some kind?* _____

_____

If you think that this change will be positive, read Episode A; if you think that this change will bring danger, read Episode B.

An Undersea Adventure with a Twist
(continued)

A Perfect Day?
Episode A

He swam deeper now. Iridescent shapes clustered in small groups brushed past him. They seemed undisturbed by his presence, and he carefully reached into his bag and drew out the camera. With a series of silent clicks, he took one, and then another photo as they swam by, their colorful bodies shimmering. Lucas smiled to himself; this was clearly going to be a special day for underwater photography. With a quick flip of his fins, he moved deeper still, toward the base of the coral reef where sea anemones beckoned gently. It was then that he noticed a black object partly buried in the sand.

1. *Circle the example of **figurative language** in this episode.*

2. *This passage contains some **sensory details**. Find and list two.* _____

_____

3. *Underline the statement which suggests that Lucas is feeling confident.*

If you think that the black object will bring Lucas good luck, read Episode C; if you think that it will bring danger, read Episode D.

A Perfect Day?
Episode B

He swam deeper now. Iridescent shapes clustered in small groups brushed past him. They seemed undisturbed by his presence, and he carefully reached into his bag and drew out the camera. With a silent click, he took one photo, then frowned as the fish suddenly became agitated and moved quickly away. "That's funny," he thought. It was only then, while he was in the process of putting his camera back in the bag, that he noticed a menacing black shape overhead.

1. *From what **point of view** is the story told?* _____

2. *Two clues in this passage **foreshadow** danger. Circle them.*

If you think that the shape is a sea creature, read Episode E; if you think the shape is not alive, read Episode F.

An Undersea Adventure with a Twist
(continued)

A Perfect Day?
Episode C

His heart beat more quickly now. From his childhood, he had heard tales of treasures discovered by chance—of entire ships uncovered or of valuable single items carried by the tide to the spot where some fortunate soul happened upon them. Even as an adult, he'd filled his bookshelves with such tales. Perhaps this was his chance! Hope flooded over him in waves, and he swam impatiently toward the object, a rush of bubbles pouring from his tank. Recklessly, he reached down, grasped the protruding end, and gave a firm pull.

1. *What two **personality traits** are characteristic of Lucas?* _____
_____

2. *What **techniques of characterization** are used by the author to make the reader aware of these traits?*
_____
_____

If you think that Lucas has found his treasure, read Episode G; if you think that he has not, read Episode H.

A Perfect Day?
Episode D

His heart beat more quickly now. There was a distinct possibility that he had come upon a moray eel. Torn between his desire for shots of the deadly creature in its natural environment and a healthy fear of the fish, he hesitated. As he did, he noticed the form begin to move. The black shape oozed forth from the sand—and was followed, to his amazement, by another form as well. Lucas's hand still held his camera. Keeping a careful eye on the creature in the sand, he began to lift his camera toward his face.

1. *What **conflict** does Lucas face at this point?* _____
2. *How does he **resolve** it?* _____
_____
_____

If you think that Lucas will safely take his pictures, read Episode I; if you think that he is endangering himself, read Episode J.

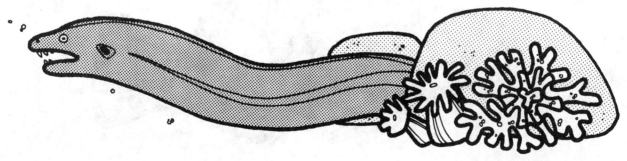

An Undersea Adventure with a Twist
(continued)

A Perfect Day?
Episode E

Lucas glanced upward, suddenly filled with a terrible foreboding. His heart beat in a frenzied rhythm, and it was only with tremendous effort that he forced himself to remain motionless—a seemingly lifeless mass among so many others on the sandy bottom. To his horror, the shape above him began to move closer, in a smoothly undulating way. Lucas watched silently for a moment, then began to inch his hand toward the spear gun hanging from his belt.

1. *What is the **mood** of this episode?* _____

_____

2. *By what means is this **mood** created?* _____

_____

If you think that the shape above Lucas will prove to be unfriendly, read Episode K; if you think that the shape will prove to be friendly, read Episode L.

A Perfect Day?
Episode F

Lucas glanced upward, suddenly frightened. Surely his float was in place! Certainly anyone who was watching would notice his silently anchored boat! Yet the triangular form continued to move steadily toward him. For one horror-stricken moment, Lucas visualized the ravenous churning of a propeller blade. At last, unable to contain himself, he forced himself onto the sandy bottom, his camera, net bag, and spear gun pressing into his side.

1. *What did Lucas think was approaching him?* _____

2. *What **clues** in the passage tell you so?* _____

_____

If you think that Lucas was correct in his identification of the shape, read Episode M; if you think that he was incorrect, read Episode N.

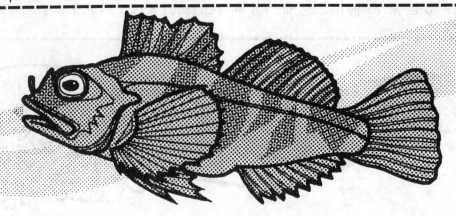

An Undersea Adventure with a Twist
(continued)

A Perfect Day?
Episode G

Nothing happened. Puzzled, Lucas paused and then once again gave a hard pull. This time he felt the object begin to move. Excitedly, he knelt and began to scoop sand from around its base. Soon he was engulfed by a cloud of fine sand particles. After ten to fifteen minutes of intense effort, he felt himself tiring. A glance at his gauge indicated that he would have to return to the surface in the next few minutes—and the object still lay embedded in sand. Frustrated, he leaned forward and peered closely at the section of black metal he had exposed. Then he saw it! A tiny 18 inscribed on the rust-covered surface. Lucas felt his heart pound. Surely this was a relic of some ancient ship. He had found his treasure! He rose, and, pulling a chart from his sea bag, recorded his location. Then, reluctantly, he began his ascent, his mind alive with thoughts of his discovery.

1. *What does the 18 **symbolize** for Lucas?* _____

2. *What is the **theme** of this story?* _____

_____

3. *What would the **theme** have been if the object had proved to be merely a piece of rusty metal?* _____

_____

A Perfect Day?
Episode H

The next thing Lucas knew, he was falling backward, for the sand had released its prey all too easily. He landed on his back, within inches of a spiny sea urchin, and the object dropped from his hand. Lucas righted himself, peered about, and with relief saw his "find" lying near him on the sandy bottom. His smile disappeared as he looked more closely, noticing for the first time the long line attached to the metal object he was now holding. With a chagrined expression, he reset his own anchor and headed for the surface.

1. *What is the author's **tone** in this last episode?* _____

_____

_____

2. *Has the **tone** been consistent throughout the story?* _____

An Undersea Adventure with a Twist
(continued)

A Perfect Day?
Episode I

As he focused the camera lens, long black arms continued to appear. He stood motionless as a large squid gradually loosened itself from the sand, hovered, and then glided slowly away. Lucas was clicking furiously now, well aware that the pictures he was taking would be a wonderful addition to his work. He smiled to himself as he thought of his apprehension earlier in the day. Then, with a glance at his air gauge, he began his easy ascent to the surface.

1. *What is the* **theme** *of this story?* _____

_____

2. *Do you feel that the conclusion is* **anticlimactic?** _____

3. *Explain your answer to question 2.* _____

_____

_____

A Perfect Day?
Episode J

He stopped when he saw the object begin to move slowly toward him, tentacles trailing behind. He stood motionless for a few, paralyzed moments, then concurred that discretion is the better part of valor. With a quick flip of his fins, he began his ascent, his camera still in his hand.

It was with great relief that he lowered himself onto the deck of his boat. "It doesn't seem possible," he thought as he glanced at his watch, "that only a few hours have passed. One thing's for sure—the next time I dive, it will be with a partner."

1. *This episode contains a* **homily,** *an often-quoted piece of advice. Write the* **homily** *here.* _____

_____

2. *Is Lucas's retreat inconsistent with the behavior pattern previously established in this story for him?* ____

3. *Name some specific* **character traits** *that support your answer to question 2.* _____

_____

_____

An Undersea Adventure with a Twist
(continued)

A Perfect Day?
Episode K

The creature was closer now, and Lucas saw at once that he was in serious trouble. It was a giant gray shark—and to Lucas it looked decidedly hungry! He pulled back on the trigger, praying that this time the gun would work correctly and not jam as it had in the past. To his relief, the spear shot out with a hiss, but it traveled past the shark and struck a large grouper hovering near the rocks. For a moment, Lucas was sure he was about to become a meal! Then suddenly, the shark turned and headed toward the wounded grouper, now struggling in its death agonies. Quickly Lucas moved upward, kicking his feet in strong rhythmic motions, trying to control the panic he was feeling. It was only when he was safely aboard the boat that he was able to stop shaking and to tell himself that he would *never* dive alone again.

1. *What is a* **moral**? _____

_____

2. *How does a* **moral** *differ from a* **theme**? _____

_____

_____

3. *If this story had a* **moral** *what might it be?* _____

_____

A Perfect Day?
Episode L

The creature swam closer, and Lucas's finger tightened. Then suddenly, with a happy flash of recognition, he heard the high-pitched squeal that only dolphins utter. He raised himself as the dolphin brushed against him, circled, and then returned. Lucas was surprised that the creature was alone; perhaps it had been separated from the school and was seeking companionship. Whatever the reason for its appearance, Lucas felt it was fortunate. Smiling, he dropped his spear gun and reached for his camera. For the next few minutes, he clicked furiously while the dolphin performed like a vaudeville-hall ham. Eventually, however, the creature tired and swam away. Lucas, too, decided it was time to leave. He repacked the camera, refastened his spear gun, and began his ascent, well pleased with the day and his unexpected find.

1. *This episode contains a* **simile**, *a form of* **figurative language** *in which one thing is compared to another. Find and circle the* **simile**.

2. *What does this* **simile** *mean?* _____

_____

_____

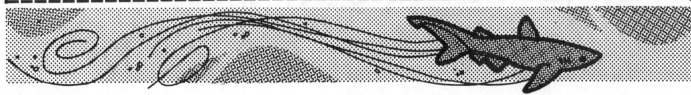

An Undersea Adventure with a Twist
(continued)

A Perfect Day?
Episode M

The shape was closer now. Lucas could actually hear the high-pitched hum of the motor and see the relentless churning of the propeller. So it *was* a boat! The entire reef had become a swirling mass of sand and bits of seaweed. Fish darted about, confused by the sound and the commotion. Then, suddenly, the boat was gone, and there was silence once again. With a sigh, Lucas raised himself off the ocean bottom and readied himself for his ascent. He couldn't understand how the boat had come so close—how it could have missed seeing not only his float, but his anchored boat as well. It was only as he broke the surface of the water and discovered that his boat was gone, that he understood at last.

*1. What is the **tone** of this episode?* _____

*2. Would the **tone** have been different if Lucas's boat had not disappeared?* _____

*3. What is the **mood** of this episode?* _____

*4. Is the **mood** of this episode consistent with the **mood** of the rest of the story?* _____

_____

A Perfect Day?
Episode N

The shape came closer until it was hovering directly over Lucas. Trembling, he forced his body closer to the sandy bottom. His heart was pounding, and his mouth opened and closed in silent cries for help. Finally, unable to bear the tension any longer, he glanced up—only to see a friendly pair of eyes peering at him from inside a face mask. It was John, a good friend, who had obviously decided to join Lucas in his dive. With an embarrassed smile, Lucas sat up, clutching a starfish in his hand. He could only hope that John, while puzzled by his interest in such an ordinary citizen of the sea, would never know the panic he had felt.

*1. What do we learn about Lucas's **character** in this episode?* _____

_____

*2. What **sensory details** does the author use to convey Lucas's panic?* _____

_____

_____

*3. What is the **tone** of this story?* _____

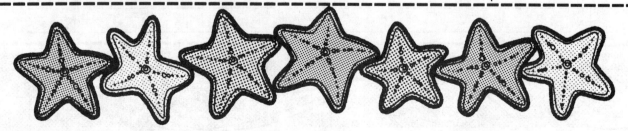

Name _____

Consider the Connotations

The **denotation** of a word is its dictionary definition, its literal meaning. The **connotation** of a word is another meaning it suggests or the shading given its literal meaning by experience or association. For example, the **denotation** of the word *renovate* is "to make new again, to renew, or to restore." The **connotations** of the word *renovate* are "to remodel," "to patch up," and "to spruce up."

The connotations of words help to determine the impact they have on us. These connotations may be positive or negative, depending on how they affect us.

Look up the meaning of each of the words listed below. Match connotations with denotations, and write the correct word on each line. The first set has been done for you.

Positive Connotation	Denotation	Negative Connotation
1. *remodeled*	1. renovated	1. *patched up*
2. _____	2. elevated	2. _____
3. _____	3. demanding	3. _____
4. _____	4. thick	4. _____
5. _____	5. distant	5. _____
6. _____	6. fanciful	6. _____
7. _____	7. unfamiliar	7. _____
8. _____	8. roomy	8. _____
9. _____	9. antiques	9. _____
10. _____	10. carefully	10. _____
11. _____	11. calm	11. _____
12. _____	12. continually	12. _____
13. _____	13. unhurried	13. _____
14. _____	14. rural	14. _____
15. _____	15. temperate	15. _____

balmy   exotic   lofty   romantic
bland   heirlooms   lush   sappy
cautiously   imposing   painstakingly slow
cavernous   incessantly   peaceful   spacious
challenging   isolated   perpetually   strange
death-defying junk   primitive   unspoiled
dull   leisurely   remote   wild

ANTIQUES **ANTIQUES** **JUNK**

Name _____

A "Remoat" Vacation

Avoid cloudy connotations. Turn this advertisement into a travel agent's dream. Select words with positive connotations from the list on page 67 and write them on the numbered lines below.

Turn your vacation into an adventure this summer. Travel to Castle in the Clouds,

an exquisitely **(1)**_____ castle perched

atop **(2)**_____ Mount Cloud. Getting there is half the fun!

You'll travel by pony cart over **(3)**_____ terrain, passing

through **(4)**_____ villages and **(5)**_____

countryside until you reach the incredibly **(6)**_____

Castle in the Clouds.

The castle itself dates from the 1300s, and is the perfect **(7)**_____

setting for a vacation with a loved one. The **(8)**_____

rooms are furnished with family **(9)**_____. The meals

are **(10)**_____, prepared **(11)**_____

by a master chef.

The pace is **(12)**_____. You'll have ample time to visit

Castle in the Cloud's **(13)**_____ surroundings. Enjoy the

view from the turret. Laugh as the **(14)**_____ breeze that

blows **(15)**_____ from the south tosses your hair.

Experience the feeling that time has passed you by.

Name _____

Do You "Sea" the Analogy?

An **analogy** is a relationship or correspondence between one pair of terms that serves as a basis for the creation of another pair. The terms in the second pair have the same relationship to each other as did the terms in the first pair. Some possible relationships are:
1. One word is an **antonym** of the other.
    Example: <u>Bow</u> is to <u>stern</u> as <u>front</u> is to <u>back</u>.
2. One word is a **kind** of the other.
    Example: <u>Sloop</u> is to <u>ship</u> as <u>sedan</u> is to <u>automobile</u>.
3. One word is a **part** of the other.
    Example: <u>Mast</u> is to <u>sailboat</u> as <u>wing</u> is to <u>airplane</u>.
4. One word is a **synonym** for the other.
    Example: <u>Sail</u> is to <u>cruise</u> as <u>fly</u> is to <u>soar</u>.

Test your ability to "sea" anologies. Write the missing term on each of the lines below.

1. A <u>star chart</u> is to a <u>sea captain</u> as a _____ is to a <u>rally driver</u>.

2. A <u>typhoon</u> is to a _____ as a <u>zephyr</u> is to a <u>wind</u>.

3. A <u>helmsman</u> is to a <u>ship</u> as a _____ is to an <u>airplane</u>.

4. <u>Aqua</u> is to <u>water</u> as <u>terra firma</u> is to _____.

5. A <u>sextant</u> is to a <u>navigator</u> as a <u>transit</u> is to a _____.

6. A <u>barometer</u> is to _____ as a <u>thermometer</u> is to <u>temperature</u>.

7. <u>Oscillate</u> is to a <u>wave</u> as <u>twinkle</u> is to a _____.

8. A <u>sea captain</u> is to the <u>sea</u> as an _____ is to <u>space</u>.

9. A <u>grain of sand</u> is to the <u>beach</u> as a <u>leaf</u> is to a _____.

10. A <u>ship's bow</u> is to its _____ as a <u>train's engine</u> is to its <u>caboose</u>.

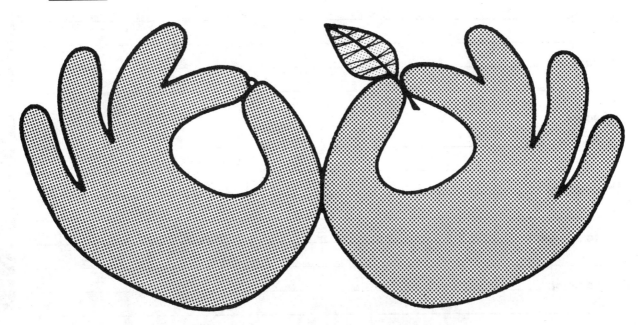

Name _____

Context Cavern

Context clues are familiar words that help the reader determine the meanings of other, unfamiliar words. There are four important kinds of context clues. In the examples of each kind given below, the word is underlined, and the context clue is set in boldface type.

1. **Restatement**—a clue provided by including a synonym or definition so that the reader is actually given the meaning of the word.
    Example: He satisfied his love of adventure by spelunking, **exploring a variety of caves** in the area.
2. **Example**—a clue provided by including examples.
    Example: A willingness to **work in confined spaces** and to **explore dark, unknown areas** is necessary for successful spelunking.
3. **Comparison**—a clue provided by comparing two seemingly unrelated things so that the meaning of one of them will be clarified.
    Example: Because he had **spent his life as a coal miner**, spelunking **held little appeal** for him.
4. **Contrast**—a clue provided by including a contrast that underscores what the word does *not* mean.
    Example: The claustrophobic gentleman was advised to try **hiking in the open air**, rather than spelunking.

For each word listed below, write four sentences that convey its meaning through context clues.

1. **cavernous**

    a. restatement: _____
    _____

    b. example: _____
    _____

    c. comparison: _____
    _____

    d. contrast: _____
    _____

2. **obscure**

    a. restatement: _____
    _____

    b. example: _____
    _____

    c. comparison: _____
    _____

    d. contrast: _____
    _____

Crafty Clues

Here's proof that the context of an unfamiliar word helps to reveal its meaning. Read this dialogue. Then write each nonsense word next to its definition on the lines below.

(Fade in. Sound of telegraph keys <u>blipstig</u> in the <u>sparcebur</u>.)

Captain Cornelius Carpenter: *(briskly)* Listen, my lad. I was <u>burneystig</u> this vast ocean long <u>zodaf</u> you were born! Do you dare to suggest that I don't <u>froster</u> how to handle my ship in a <u>waterwam</u> of this magnitude?

Miles Frost, the telegrapher: Certainly not, sir. The fact remains, however, that <u>Listermat</u> Bob Ritter of the *Sea Long* reports <u>sleever</u> winds gusting to 85 knots and rough seas ahead. In iceberg country, that's pretty <u>mordeldow</u> business at best.

(Sound of a <u>zurup</u>, crashing screech.)

Captain Carpenter: What in the world…?

Miles: *(in a <u>crosbean</u> whisper)* I think, Captain, that our <u>brarney</u> fears are being realized.

Captain Carpenter: <u>Breden</u>, send an SOS while there's still <u>sooley</u>. I'm off to the bridge.

(Sound of door <u>drastig</u> and footsteps fading into the <u>sparcebur</u>. Frantic <u>blipstig</u> of <u>schloodle</u> keys.)

1. background _____
2. before _____
3. clicking _____
4. closing _____
5. dangerous _____
6. first mate _____
7. high _____
8. hushed _____

9. know _____
10. loud _____
11. quick _____
12. sailing _____
13. storm _____
14. telegraph _____
15. time _____
16. worst _____

Name _____

Jungle Trackdown

You have been asked to write a guidebook to aid fellow explorers in recognizing and identifying these "inhabitants" of jungles and tropical forests. Use a dictionary to help you describe each one.

1. liana _____

2. piranha _____

3. tapir _____

4. curassow _____

5. tinamou _____

6. calabash _____

7. fer-de-lance _____

8. caiman _____

9. buriti _____

10. bittern _____

11. anaconda _____

12. sloth _____

13. bushmaster _____

14. macaw _____

15. coati _____

Your guidebook will be divided into sections. There will be separate listings for plants, fish, birds, reptiles, and mammals. On the lines below each section title, write in alphabetical order the names of the "inhabitants" that will be described in that section.

Plants	**Birds**	**Reptiles**	**Mammals**
_____	_____	_____	_____
_____	_____	_____	_____
_____	_____	_____	_____
	_____	_____	

Fish

_____

Name _____

Homonym Hang-up

> **Homonyms** are words that sound alike but have different meanings. For example, the noun *quail* and the verb *quail* are homonyms, and the words *sea* and *see* are homonyms.

On the lines below, write pairs of sentences using homonyms. Underline the homonyms in each sentence pair. The first pair has been done for you.

1. a. <u>She climbed to the mountain peak</u>. _____
   b. <u>You will see if you peek</u>. _____
2. a. _____
   b. _____
3. a. _____
   b. _____
4. a. _____
   b. _____
5. a. _____

   b. _____
6. a. _____

   _____

   _____

6. b. _____

   _____

7. a. _____

   _____

   b. _____

   _____

Name _____

Hang in There

> Words with **multiple meanings** can be used in more than one way. For example, the word *run* is used in four different ways when we speak of a home *run,* a *run* in a stocking, and a *run* on a bank, or when we *run* home.

Get the jump on words with multiple meanings. For each word held aloft by a parachute, write three sentences. Use the word in a different way in each sentence.

1. a. _____
   b. _____
   c. _____

2. a. _____
   b. _____
   c. _____

3. a. _____
   b. _____
   c. _____

4. a. _____
   b. _____
   c. _____

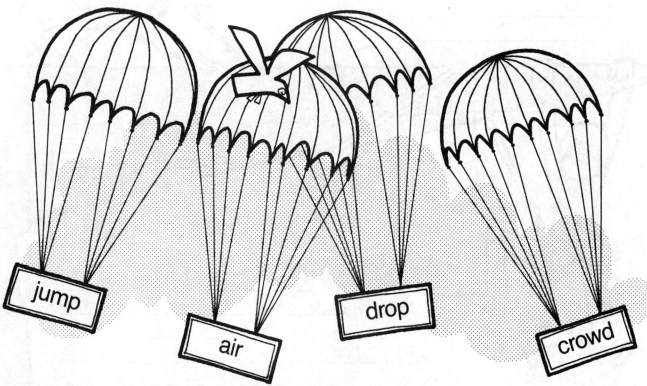

Name _____

The Etymology Express

Etymology is the systematic study of linguistic forms, such as words. An **etymologist** studies the origins and parts of words. Many words have several parts. These words actually consist of a base or root word to which prefixes and/or suffixes have been added. A **prefix** is a word part that is added to the front of a base word to change its meaning. A **suffix** is a word part that is added to the end of a base word to change its meaning. When a suffix is added, the part of speech is usually changed. Sometimes, the spelling of the base word must be changed as well.

The engine below contains prefixes, the coal car contains base words, and the caboose carries suffixes. Hook these base words and word parts together to create different words. Write the words you create on the lines provided. To calculate your score, look up your creations in a dictionary. Give yourself five points for each word part you used correctly. Total your score on the track to the right.

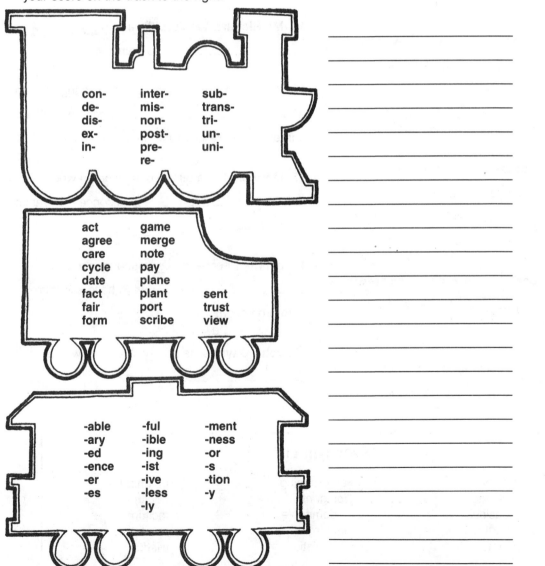

con-	inter-	sub-
de-	mis-	trans-
dis-	non-	tri-
ex-	post-	un-
in-	pre-	uni-
	re-	

act	game	
agree	merge	
care	note	
cycle	pay	
date	plane	
fact	plant	sent
fair	port	trust
form	scribe	view

-able	-ful	-ment
-ary	-ible	-ness
-ed	-ing	-or
-ence	-ist	-s
-er	-ive	-tion
-es	-less	-y
	-ly	

Name _____

Cast About for a Synonym

As the novelist, Pearl E. Prose, you have just begun a fictional account of the sinking of the *Titanic*. You are now making a list of the characters you will include—and they certainly constitute a varied group! Complete the brief description that follows each name by writing a synonym for the underlined adjective on the nearby line.

1. **Professor I.Q.**—a <u>quiet</u> scholar with a

_____ personality.

2. **Patricia Nomen**—a <u>hopeful</u> spinster whose

_____ looks drive men away.

3. **Emily Vanderpill**—a <u>poor</u> relation of Richard Vanderpill's; a woman whose shabby clothes betray

her _____ life.

4. **Joy Rox**—a <u>cheerful</u> young woman with an

_____ outlook on life.

5. **Dan Dodge**—a <u>rebellious</u> and

_____ young man.

6. **Mrs . Erma Smug**—a woman whose <u>unconquerable</u> confidence and

_____ air make it difficult to

tolerate her for long periods of time.

7. **Mrs. Ann Cognito**— a <u>mysterious</u> widow whose

_____ smile puzzles those

around her.

8. **Mr. Ron Dare**—a <u>bold</u> young man whose

_____ approach gives others

confidence.

9. **Miss Ida Care**—an <u>indifferent</u> young woman

whose_____ attitude toward

things around her is especially annoying to Mrs.

Smug.

10. **Captain Waiver**—the <u>indecisive</u> captain of the

ship; a man whose _____

mind renders him incapable of making decisions.

11. **Mr. Richard Vanderpill**—a <u>wealthy</u>,

_____ financier.

12. **Abigale A. Lone**—a <u>resourceful</u> young woman

whose _____ schemes often

border on the illegal or the unscrupulous.

13. **Mary Meek**—a <u>pitiful</u> young woman whose

_____ looks conceal a brain of

limited capacity.

14. **Jimmy Peece**—a <u>lazy</u> young man whose

_____ ways have kept him

from promotion.

15. **John Gaynes**—a <u>sporty</u> salesman with a

_____ grin.

Synonym List

affluent	enterprising	poignant
apathetic	indigent	rakish
audacious	indomitable	taciturn
defiant	lethargic	vacillating
enigmatic	optimistic	wistful

Name _____

Pack a Thesaurus

Don't be caught unprepared on your next creative outing. Pack along a thesaurus, and watch your writing come alive! Read the paragraph below. Then, open your pack, use your thesaurus to find a synonym for each word in List A, and write these synonyms on the numbered lines to complete the paragraph.

(1) _____ Mountain was aptly named, for it did, indeed, overlook the valley below. Water gushed through the long **(2)** _____ that **(3)** _____ the valley floor, its journey clearly audible in the still mountain air. The young **(4)** _____ began his climb. He knew the **(5)** _____ that lay ahead of him. The **(6)** _____ was steep, with a long, **(7)** _____ face where footholds were few. Yet he was an **(8)** _____ young man, and he began with an air of **(9)** _____. He hoped to reach the **(10)** _____ before night, because it would provide protection from the approaching snowstorm. He paused, imagining himself planting his flag atop the **(11)** _____, a small **(12)** _____ to those who had attempted the **(13)** _____ before him. For a moment he stood, panting, on a **(14)** _____ that jutted out from the slope. Then, with a determined look, he continued his **(15)** _____ climb.

List A

1. lookout
2. ravine
3. crossed
4. climber
5. dangers
6. slope
7. vertical
8. adventurous
9. defiance
10. refuge
11. peak
12. memorial
13. climb
14. cliff
15. difficult

Synonyms

1. s _ _ _ _ _ _ _
2. c _ _ _ _
3. t _ _ _ _ _ _ _
4. a _ _ _ _ _ _ _
5. h _ _ _ _ _
6. i _ _ _ _ _ _
7. s _ _ _ _ _
8. e _ _ _ _ _ _ _
9. b _ _ _ _ _ _
10. c _ _ _ _ _ _
11. p _ _ _ _ _ _ _
12. t _ _ _ _ _ _
13. a _ _ _ _ _
14. p _ _ _ _ _ _ _
15. a _ _ _ _ _

Name _____

How's That Again, Pardner?

Tales of the Old West and late-night westerns are filled with stock phrases ("No man calls me a liar and lives, stranger!") that have long since become clichés. Ikin Direct, the famous European film maker, has decided to make a western, but a western with class. Using a thesaurus, he has rephrased ten western clichés to give them a loftier tone. Somehow, though, he seems to have missed the point. Use a thesaurus and/or a dictionary to find the clichés Ikin Direct has obfuscated with his lofty language.

1. Lift your upper limbs and hold them aloft!

_____

2. Intersect them at the gap.

_____

3. Seek sanctuary! It is an ambuscade!

_____

4. They will never apprehend me animated.

_____

5. There is bullion in those hummocks.

_____

6. Extend your hands toward the firmament.

_____

7. It is an abominable twenty-four-hour period at Ebony Megalith.

_____

8. It is exhilarating to be in habitation on the open land once more.

_____

9. We are encompassed!

_____

10. Advance in a westerly direction, juvenile sir.

_____

DESIST!

The Action and Adventure News

On the lines below, begin a newspaper article based on the book you have just read. Write any type of article you feel is appropriate—a news story, a feature story, a sports story, an editorial, or a column. Continue your article on a separate sheet of paper if necessary. Your finished article will be grouped with articles written by other students in this class to create an edition of the *Action and Adventure News.*

Boy Saves Child From Burning Building

A **news story** usually answers the questions who, what, when, where, why, and how. These questions are answered in the first paragraph of the story, which is called the **lead**. The information that follows the lead is organized according to its importance so that later paragraphs in the story can be cut to make the story fit available page space without eliminating any of the essential facts.

Local Surfer Trains Hard

A **feature story** is a human interest story. It does not begin by answering questions. Instead, it opens with some sort of attention-getting statement. As the story progresses, details are added to develop the piece and to lead to a conclusion that will involve the reader emotionally and/or get him or her to respond in some way.

Burners Whip Hawks

A **sports story** usually describes the outcome of an athletic competition of some sort in words that recreate for the reader some of the atmosphere and excitement of the actual contest.

Vote for John Smith

An **editorial** is written to convince readers to adopt a particular point of view and/or to take some particular action. In a well-written editorial, a problem is defined, facts about it are presented, and a solution is proposed. Was there an issue in your book that could become the subject of an editorial?

Dear Edna...

One kind of article is a question-and-answer **column.** For this type of column, you would need to create letters of questions and responses based on important concerns expressed in the book you have just read.

_____

_____

_____

_____

_____

_____

When you have finished writing your article, create a **nameplate** that could be used for the *Action and Adventure News.* Include the name of the paper, a slogan or saying that represents it, and a design that symbolizes this illustrious journal.

A Bird's-Eye View of Books

Title	Main Characters	Setting	Type of Conflict	Climax	Point of View	Theme

Action Readers' Panel

> Will the real reader please stand up? One real reader and two impostors attempt to stump a panel of questioners in this fun-filled activity.

Materials Needed

two tables
six chairs

Instructions

Before Class

1. Have each student read a different book.
2. Place two tables at the front of the room and put three chairs at each table.

During Class

1. Group the students in teams of three.
2. Tell the members of one team that they are to be the readers. They are to meet as a group and decide which one of the three books they have collectively read will be used for this activity. After they have selected a book, the team member who actually read that book is to give the other members of his team as much information about the book as he can in the time provided.
3. Tell members of another team that they are to serve as the panel of questioners.
4. Ask members of the reading team to be seated at one table and members of the questioning panel to be seated at the other table.
5. Tell panel members that they are to question members of the reading team in an effort to determine which team member *actually* read the book. They are to take turns and may ask their questions of any team member but must specify by number which team member they are addressing. Panelists may each ask three questions before they must cast their votes for reading team member 1, 2, or 3.
6. After all of the votes have been cast, ask the real reader to please stand up.
7. If the reading team has succeeded in stumping the panel, give each team member one point for a team total of three. If the panel correctly identifies the real reader, give each panel member who guessed correctly one point.
8. Continue this activity until members of each team have had an opportunity to serve as readers and as questioners.

Follow-up

Have the members of each team create an advertisement, brochure, dust jacket, or poster for their book.

Name _____

Action and Adventure Class-It

Work against the clock! The letters in the word **action** provide the categories for this exercise. How many words starting with each letter can you find that are related to the outdoor activities listed on the left? Use all of the reference materials available to you, and see if you can fill in the squares in thirty minutes.

Outdoor Activity	A	C	T	I	O	N
spelunking		cave				
hang gliding						
surfing						
parachuting						
skin diving						
mountain climbing						

Name _____

Party Time

It's party time, and you are planning a gala based on an adventure theme.

1. Select an adventurous career.

☐ archaeologist   ☐ parachutist
☐ arctic explorer   ☐ paramedic
☐ big game hunter   ☐ single-handed sailor
☐ deep-sea fisherman   ☐ skin diver
☐ forest ranger   ☐ spelunker
☐ jungle explorer   ☐ test pilot
☐ long-distance swimmer ☐ other: _____

2. Design an invitation.

3. Plan a menu.

Name _____

Party Time
(continued)

4. On the lines below, describe the decorations you will use.

_____

_____

_____

_____

_____

5. In the space below, describe or sketch and label some of the costumes you and your guests will wear.

6. On the lines below, list the games and activities you have selected to amuse your guests.

_____

_____

_____

_____

_____

_____

Don't Just Say It—Portray It!

1. Choose one of the statements in the box below.
2. On a separate sheet of paper, illustrate the statement you have chosen.
3. Select a sentence from a story you have read.
4. On a separate sheet of paper, illustrate the sentence you have selected.

> • His parachute collapsed suddenly.
> • Toes gripping the board, she sped through the water.
> • Molten lava flowed rapidly toward the village.
> • After the engine sputtered and died, the plane dropped slowly at first and then more rapidly toward the earth.
> • Coming into the curve too rapidly, the toboggan rode high on the sidewall and then left the course.

Name _____

Action-Filled Figure Poem

1. Decide on an experience about which you wish to write.
2. On the back of this page or on a separate sheet of paper, list sensory details and vivid expressions that relate to this experience.
3. Work with the words you have listed until you have created a few descriptive lines.
4. In the space below, sketch a picture of an object that is related to the experience you selected.
5. Write the descriptive lines around the outline of this object.

SIZZLING THUNDEROUS VELVETY CAREENING

FADED ICY SILENT SMOLDERING HAIRY

GRIM SILVERY DAMP PRICKLY FIZZING

CLAMMY DAPPLED SHRIEKING OILY MELLOW

Caution—Misplaced Modifier Ahead!

Once you have illustrated a misplaced modifier, you'll be on the lookout for them in your writing. The sentence below is a good example.

The fireman watched for the burning house racing down the street.

Select one of the sentences below. On a separate sheet of paper, illustrate the misplaced modifier. Then, on the lines provided, rewrite each sentence to correct the order and clarify the meaning.

1. The sky diver leaped from the top of the tall building carrying a parachute.

_____

_____

2. The climber discovered a hidden cave rappelling from a mountain peak.

_____

_____

3. The hunters sought shelter beneath a tree dazed by the unrelenting sun.

_____

_____

4. The explorers examined the map sitting by the campfire.

_____

_____

5. The canoe hit a rock shooting through the rapids.

_____

_____

Action Adverbs

This exercise should go *winningly* for you if you focus *sharply* on the examples below.

"I love mountain climbing," he said *loftily*.
"I've lost sight of the target," he said *aimlessly*.
"I love downhill skiing," she said *slalomly*.
"My feelings about the expedition are divided," she said *half-heartedly*.

Supply appropriate adverbs for these statements.

1. "This is an incredible story," the captain commented _____.

2. "There are rapids just ahead," she announced _____.

3. "This mountain is very steep," the climber observed _____.

4. "Lower the periscope," he commanded _____.

5. "It's a hidden cave," she exclaimed _____.

Then, supply appropriate statements for these adverbs.

6. "_____,"
_____ *tremulously*.

7. "_____,"
_____ *pointedly*.

8. "_____,"
_____ *searingly*.

9. "_____,"
_____ *searchingly*.

10. "_____,"
_____ *painfully*.

Finally, on the lines below, create some action adverb statements of your own, and share them with a friend.

_____

_____

_____

_____

_____

Name _____

The Action and Adventure Hit Parade

As the famous music critic, S. Ournotes, you write a weekly column featuring the hit tunes. This week, however, the music company failed to send you a list of the songs that "made the charts." As a result, you'll have to create them. Let your imagination go as you fill in the titles and performers for hits in the classical, rock, and country and western categories.

Classical

"Antarctic Étude" by the Richard Byrd Chamber Group

"Raft Racing Rhapsody" by the Floaters

_____

_____

_____

_____

Rock

"Shake That Pan" by the Nuggets

"Submarine Stomp" by the Deep-Sea Six

_____

_____

_____

_____

Country and Western

"Hold on to That Boulder, Honey, It's Comin' Down Tonight" by the Climbers

"I'm All Alone on the Sea in the Night" by Solo Sailor

_____

_____

_____

_____

Action-Packed Ads

Camera Script

Distance shot: Jungle explorer trudging wearily through the bush followed by fifty exhausted bearers.

Close-up: Explorer's face, expression grim, brow furrowed, eyes scanning the terrain ahead.

Distance shot: A small group of men gathered about a fire.

Medium shot: A person standing in a large, black kettle that is resting on a fire.

Close-up: Pot's occupant, with sweat pouring from brow, wearing an anxious expression and continually glancing at a watch (waterproof, of course).

Medium shot: Explorer and bearers as they approach the edge of a clearing.

Close-up: Person in pot, eyes bright, huge smile on face, right arm outstretched.

Close-up: Smiling jungle explorer, likewise with right arm outstretched, and with a bottle in right hand.

Close-up: Explorer's hand, then zoom to bottle.

(**Voice over:** Hot-Stop, the drink that stops your thirst cold!)

Final: Bearers, explorer, natives, and person in pot cheerfully smiling and drinking Hot-Stop.

Add a little action to advertising. Select any adventure-packed situation (rafting through rapids, swimming the English Channel, rappelling from a mountain), and use it as the lead-in for a commercial to advertise a product you create. On a separate sheet of paper, write a camera script like the one above. Then, if possible, use video equipment to tape your commercial.

Name _____

Concoct a Cartoon

You have been chosen by the well-known newspaper publisher, I. C. Print, to create a new cartoon character, a hero or heroine whose adventurous exploits will captivate the reading public. You are, of course, overwhelmed; but you need not panic. Just follow the simple steps listed below to achieve cartoon fame and fortune.

1. Create a cartoon hero or heroine. You may wish to base him or her on a character in a story you have read. Write the character's name and brief description on the lines below.

   _____
   _____
   _____
   _____
   _____

2. Assign the character some definite personality traits. Remember that this is a hero or heroine and should be slightly "larger than life." List some of your character's most unusual or outstanding traits on the lines below.

   _____
   _____
   _____
   _____
   _____
   _____
   _____
   _____
   _____
   _____
   _____
   _____
   _____
   _____
   _____
   _____

3. Decide on the physical appearance of your character. Be sure that it is in keeping with the personality you have created. Draw a picture of your character here.

Concoct a Cartoon
(continued)

4. Plan the initial episode in which you will introduce your character to the public. List the sequence of events in this episode or describe it on the lines below.

_____

_____

_____

_____

_____

_____

_____

_____

_____

_____

_____

_____

5. In the boxes below, draw the first six frames of your cartoon strip. Continue the strip on a separate sheet of paper, adding frames until the episode is complete.

Hunt a Word

Twenty-four action and adventure words are listed below. Some of these words could have been made from the letters in the words **action and adventure**, and some of them could not. Underline the words that could *not* have been made from the letters in the words **action and adventure**.

cavern	extend	traction
danger	motion	trade
dare	ration	travel
dictation	read	tread
divert	redirect	true
endure	rescue	uneven
entice	taciturn	vacant
event	tent	vacation

Hundreds of other words can be made from these letters. List some of them on the lines below. Remember that each of the eighteen letters can be used only once in any one word.

_____   _____
_____   _____
_____   _____
_____   _____
_____   _____
_____   _____
_____   _____
_____   _____
_____   _____
_____   _____
_____   _____
_____   _____
_____   _____

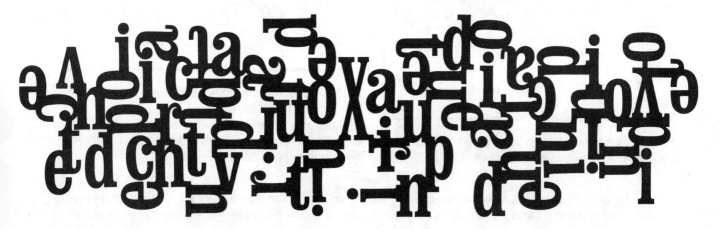

Name _____

Signpost Summaries

In the plot summary below, the author has used signposts to indicate the dangers that Hoss Willard encounters during an afternoon on the trail, rather than expressing them verbally. Read this summary.

Hoss Willard rode confidently out of town that afternoon, certain that he would find the treasure. His first indication that things would not go smoothly came about ten minutes later.

"Oh well," he thought as he pulled on his poncho, "things are sure to improve."

Hoss continued cheerfully on his way, unaware that the path on which he rode led to disaster.

He checked his horse just in time and veered off to the left where the ground was more firm.

The path was becoming steeper and more treacherous now. Hoss picked his way along the rocky trail carefully, but suddenly

He pulled up sharply on his horse's reins and narrowly escaped rolling disaster.

Hoss continued on his way, more apprehensively now, sensing that somehow this was *not* going to be his day. He was right.

Pulling his gun from his holster, Hoss fired quickly. Fortunately, he hit his target.

Hoss paused and then, with a sigh, decided that enough was enough. Climbing down from his horse, he began to pitch camp.

On a separate sheet of paper, write your own signpost summary. Base it on a story you've read or created. Summarize the tale in six to eight sentences, and use signposts to alert the reader to the dangers that lie ahead.

Name _____

Adventure in Listening

Cut off the bottom part of this page and hand it to a partner. Ask him or her to read the instructions to you slowly and to say each instruction only once. Have ready a pencil and red, orange, yellow, green, and black crayons or marking pens. Listen carefully and follow the instructions.

1. Color the flippers black, the mask red, and the tank orange.

2. In the upper right-hand corner of the frame, draw a green turtle.

3. Just above the diver's tank, draw a fish and color it the same color as the mask.

4. With your pencil, draw five air bubbles rising above the diver's head.

5. Draw a starfish in front of the diver's mask. Color it to match the tank.

6. Draw a yellow octopus shaking hands with the diver.

7. Put some green sea grass beneath the diver's left flipper.

8. With your pencil, draw four pebbles beneath the swimmer's right knee and two below his left flipper.

9. If there are four air bubbles in the picture, put an **x** in the bottom left-hand corner of the frame. If there are five air bubbles, put a circle in the bottom right-hand corner.

10. Using the same color you used for the flippers, put your first initial on the air tank and your last initial on the mask.

Name _____

Good News/Bad News

The same news can be good or bad, depending on where you are and how you look at it, and there may be humor in an unexpected twist. Read the good news/bad news sentence pairs below. Then, on the lines below, create ten similar pairs to share with your friends.

The good news was that my parachute worked.
The bad news was that I was still on the ground.

The good news was that the lost man was found.
The bad news was that it was a bear that found him.

The good news was that I was on the cresting wave.
The bad news was that my board was on the beach.

1. _____
_____

2. _____
_____

3. _____
_____

4. _____
_____

5. _____
_____

6. _____
_____

7. _____
_____

8. _____
_____

9. _____
_____

10. _____
_____

Name _____

Shades-of-Meaning Spectra

Below are pairs of words that are related in concept but opposite in meaning. It is possible to place words between the members of each pair so that the meaning is changed gradually from one extreme to the other. Write words on the lines between these antonyms so that the transition from one end of the meaning spectrum to the other is gradual. Use a dictionary or thesaurus to help you understand shades of meaning. The first one has been done for you.

1. cold	*cool*	*tepid*	*warm*	hot
2. dangerous				safe
3. depressed				exhilarated
4. ethereal				substantial
5. foolish				wise
6. futile				worthwhile
7. innocuous				fatal
8. murky				clear
9. ravishing				hideous
10. vilify				eulogize

Name _____

Forlorn Feet

These two feet have been abused by their owner. What happened to them? Where have they been? Create a dialogue between them.

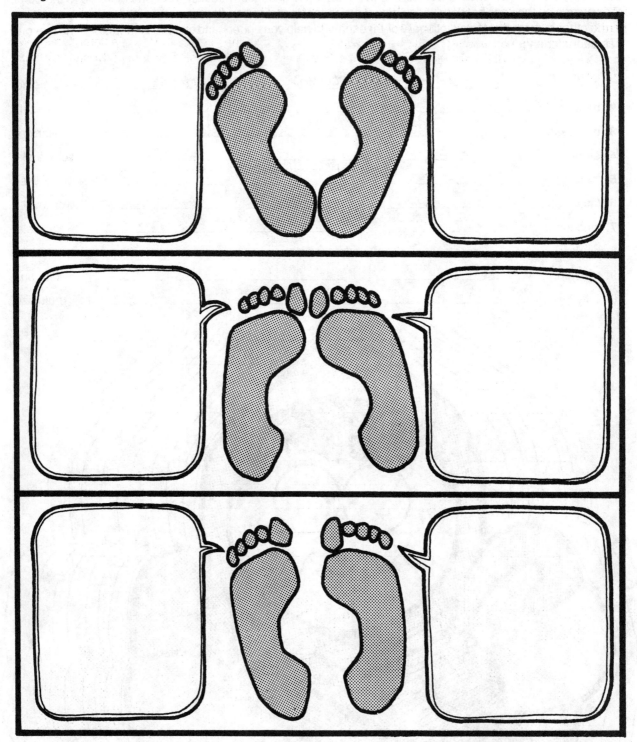

On a separate sheet of paper, write the conversation between these feet in paragraph form. Remember to use quotation marks to show which foot—the left or the right—is speaking.

An Adventure in Limerick

The **limerick** is a humorous, five-line poem that follows a definite rhyme pattern and has a particular rhythm. In a limerick, lines 1, 2, and 5 each have three feet (that is, three stressed, or accented, syllables) and rhyme with one another; and lines 3 and 4 each have only two feet and rhyme with each other. This poetic form gets its name from Limerick, Ireland, where it may have originated.

Read these limericks about adverturesome souls. Then, on the lines below, write two different limericks about a surfer named Sue, a skin diver named Amos, a spelunker called Sven, or some other adventurer of your own invention.

There once was a climber named Bill
Who fell very fast down a hill.
"Don't move me," said he,
"For I've smashed my left knee,
And think that I'd rather stay still."

A parachute jumper named Kate,
Made her first and last jump out of state.
When the chute didn't open.
She just kept a-hopin',
But ended up flat as a plate!

_____

_____

_____

_____

_____

_____

_____

_____

_____

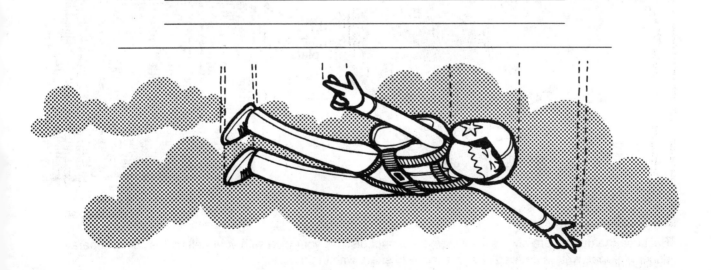

Escape!

This is it! After three years in an enemy prison camp, you are ready to make your escape; but it won't be easy! You must overcome these five obstacles:

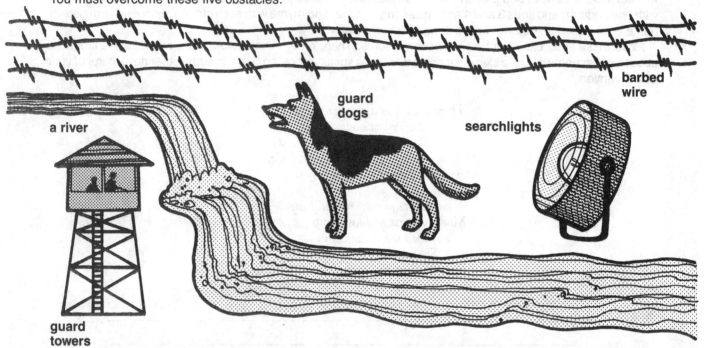

barbed wire

a river

guard dogs

searchlights

guard towers

Your only tools are

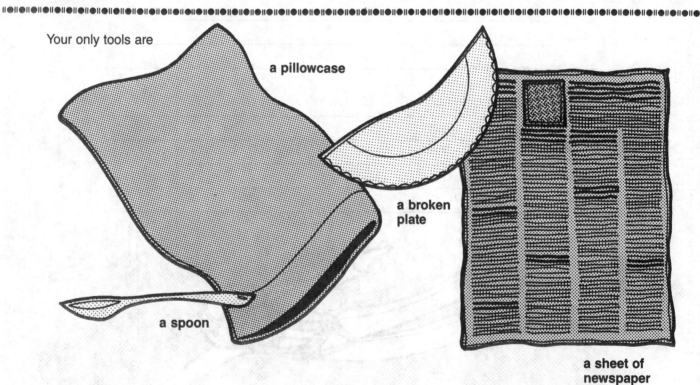

a pillowcase

a broken plate

a spoon

a sheet of newspaper

Because the guards are always listening, you cannot discuss your plan with your cell mates. On a separate sheet of paper, write a detailed plan of escape to share with them.

Action and Adventure Bibliography

Adamson, Joy. *Born Free: The Story of a Lioness of Two Worlds.* New York: Pantheon, 1960. Grade 9 and up.

_____. *Forever Free.* New York: Harcourt, Brace & World, 1962.

_____. *The Story of Elsa.* New York: Pantheon Books, 1966.

Bierce, Ambrose. *An Occurrence at Owl Creek Bridge.* Creative's Classics Series. Mankato, Minn.: Creative Education, 1980. Grades 4-9.

Byrd, Richard E. *Discovery: The Story of the Second Byrd Antarctic Expedition.* Reprint of 1935 edition. Detroit, Mich.: Gale Research Company, 1971.

Cavanna, Betty. *Runaway Voyage.* New York: William Morrow, 1978. Grades 7-9.

_____. *Spice Island Mystery.* New York: William Morrow, 1969. Grade 7 and up.

_____. *The Surfer and the City Girl.* Philadelphia, Pa.: Westminster Press, 1981. Grades 7-9.

Douglas, William O. *Of Men and Mountains.* Seattle, Wash.: Seattle Book Company, 1981.

Dumas, Alexandre. "Escape by Sea." In *Short Stories.* Index Reprint Series. Reprint of 1927 edition. Salem, N.H.: Ayer Company, n.d.

Frank, Anne. *Anne Frank: The Diary of a Young Girl.* Translated from the Dutch by B. M. Mooyaart-Doubleday with an introduction by Eleanor Roosevelt. Revised edition. Garden City, N.Y.: Doubleday, 1967.

Harkins, Philip. *The Day of the Drag Race.* New York: William Morrow, 1960. Grade 7 and up.

Harte, Bret. "The Luck of Roaring Camp." In *The Luck of Roaring Camp and Other Sketches.* Boston, Mass.: Houghton Mifflin, n.d.

_____. *The Luck of Roaring Camp,* edited by Walter Pauk and Raymond Harris. Jamestown Classics Series. Providence, R.I.: Jamestown, 1976. Grades 6-12.

Heyerdahl, Thor. *Aku-Aku: The Secret of Easter Island.* Chicago, Ill.: Rand McNally, 1958.

_____. *Kon-Tiki: Across the Pacific by Raft.* Translated by F. H. Lyon. Chicago, Ill.: Rand McNally, 1950.

Kipling, Rudyard. "Rikki-Tikki-Tavi." In *Captains Courageous and Other Stories.* New York: Dodd, Mead, 1959.

Action and Adventure Bibliography
(continued)

London, Jack. *The Best Short Stories of Jack London.* New York: Doubleday, 1953.

_____. *To Build a Fire.* Creative's Classics Series. Mankato, Minn.: Creative Education, 1980. Grades 4-9.

_____. *The Law of Life,* edited by Walter Pauk and Raymond Harris. Jamestown Classics Series. Providence, R.I.: Jamestown, 1976. Grades 6-12.

_____. "The White Silence." In *The Call of the Wild and Other Stories.* New York: Grosset and Dunlap, n.d.

Meader, Stephen W. *Whaler Round the Horn.* New York: Harcourt Brace Jovanovich, 1950. Grades 7-9.

Paine, Albert B. *The Adventures of Mark Twain.* Reprint of the 1915 edition. Darby, Pa.: Darby Books, 1981.

Rathjen, Carl H. *Mystery at Smoke River.* Mount Vernon, N.Y.: Lantern Press, 1968. Grades 6-10.

Sperry, Armstrong. *Call It Courage.* New York: Macmillan, 1971. Grades 5-7.

Twain, Mark. *The Adventures of Huckleberry Finn.* New York: Bantam Books, n.d. Grades 7-12.

_____. *The Adventures of Tom Sawyer.* New York: Bantam Books, n.d. Grade 7 and up.

_____. *Complete Short Stories,* edited by Charles Neider. Bantam Books, n.d. Grade 8 and up.

Ullman, James Ramsey. *And Not to Yield.* Garden City, N.Y.: Doubleday, 1970.

_____. *Banner in the Sky: The Story of a Boy and a Mountain.* New York: Harper & Row, 1954.

_____. *The White Tower.* Philadelphia, Pa.: J. B. Lippincott, 1945.

Reading Skills Checklist

List students' last names on the lines at the left. When a skill is introduced, draw a diagonal line through the corresponding box and shade the upper portion. When that same skill is mastered, shade the remaining portion of the box.

Names	Vocabulary											Literal Comprehension							Interpretive Comprehension				Literary Terms											
	Analogies	Antonyms	Connotation/Denotation	Context Clues	Dictionary Skills	Homonyms	Multiple Meanings	Prefixes	Suffixes	Synonyms	Thesaurus	Comparison/Contrast	Fact or Opinion	Locating Information	Main Idea	Recognizing Author's Purpose	Sequencing	Supporting Details	Cause and Effect	Drawing Conclusions	Making Inferences	Point of View	Antagonist/Protagonist	Characterization	Climax	Conflict	Figurative Language	Flashback	Foreshadowing	Mood	Plot	Setting	Symbol	Theme	Tone

Shoot for the Stars!

Man's greatest adventure may still be ahead of him—the conquest of space. Using a story you have read in class, shoot for the stars by demonstrating your understanding of the skills you have practiced in this action and adventure unit. Write your answers in the spaces provided on pages 106-107. If a question is not applicable to the story you have read, write **N/A** beside the question number on your paper.

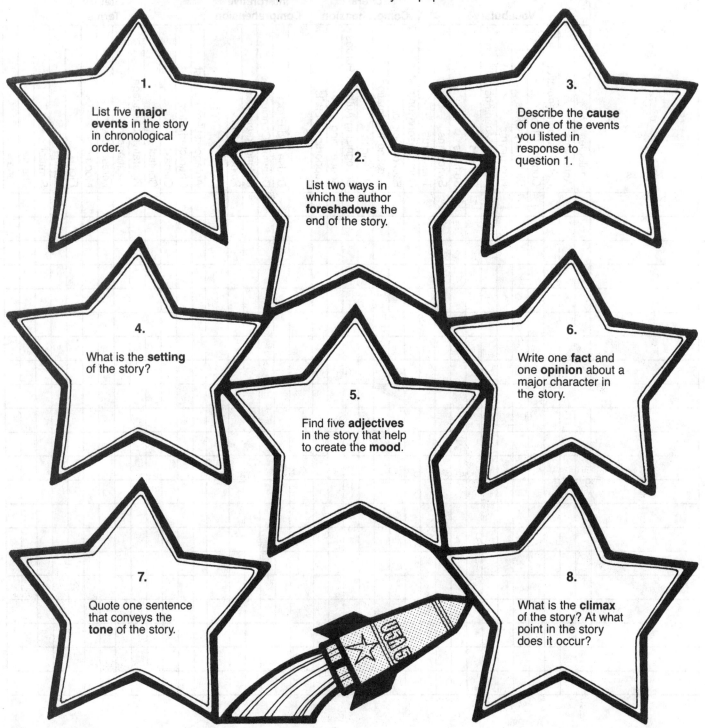

1. List five **major events** in the story in chronological order.

2. List two ways in which the author **foreshadows** the end of the story.

3. Describe the **cause** of one of the events you listed in response to question 1.

4. What is the **setting** of the story?

5. Find five **adjectives** in the story that help to create the **mood**.

6. Write one **fact** and one **opinion** about a major character in the story.

7. Quote one sentence that conveys the **tone** of the story.

8. What is the **climax** of the story? At what point in the story does it occur?

Shoot for the Stars!
(continued)

9.
What is the major **conflict** in the story? How is it resolved?

10.
From what **point of view** is the story told? By whom?

11.
List three **personality traits** of a major character and tell how the author made you aware of these traits.

12.
Name two characteristics of the **protagonist** that set him or her at odds with the **antagonist**.

13.
What can you **infer** about the title the author selected for the story?

14.
What was the **author's purpose** in writing this story?

15.
Compare the way the major character thinks and acts at the beginning of the story with the way he or she thinks and acts at the end.

16.
What example of **symbolism** can you find in this story?

17.
Give two examples of **figurative language** used in the story.

Name _____

Shoot for the Stars!
(continued)

sequencing/plot
(pp. 19-20, 21-22)

1. a. _____
   b. _____
   c. _____
   d. _____
   e. _____

foreshadowing
(pp. 48, 49)

2. a. _____
   b. _____

cause and effect
(pp. 25, 26)

3. _____
   _____

setting
(pp. 52, 53)

4. *time* _____
   place _____

mood
(pp. 50-51)

5. a. _____   c. _____
   b. _____   d. _____

   e. _____

fact or opinion
(pp. 11-12)

6. *fact* _____
   _____
   opinion _____
   _____

tone
(pp. 56, 57, 58)

7. _____
   _____

climax
(p. 43)

8. a. _____
   _____
   b. _____
   _____

conflict
(pp. 41, 42)

9. a. _____
   b. _____
   _____

point of view
(pp. 33, 34)

10. a. _____
    b. _____

characterization
(pp. 36, 37, 38, 39-40)

11. a. _____
    _____
    b. _____
    _____
    c. _____
    _____

Name _____

Shoot for the Stars!
(continued)

antagonist/
protagonist
(p. 35)

12. **a.** _____

b. _____

making inferences
(pp. 31, 32)

13. _____
_____

author's purpose
(pp. 17, 18)

14. _____
_____

compare and
contrast
(p. 10)

15. _____
_____
_____
_____

symbol
(p. 54)

16. _____
_____

figurative
language
(pp. 44, 45)

17. **a.** _____
_____

b. _____
_____

Read each question below. Then write the correct answer on the numbered line.

18. Complete the following **analogy**: <u>Disaster</u> is to <u>calamity</u> as <u>refuge</u> is to

18. _____

19. Write a **synonym** for <u>precarious</u>.

19. _____

20. Write an **antonym** for <u>timid</u>.

20. _____

21. "The <u>run</u> on first-aid equipment left the expedition without sufficient medical supplies." What is the meaning of the underlined word in this sentence?

21. _____
_____
_____

22. What is the meaning of the **prefix** con- in such words as <u>conform</u> and <u>convene</u>?

22. _____

23. What is the meaning of the **suffix** -ist in such words as <u>artist</u>, <u>balloonist</u>, and <u>novelist</u>?

23. _____
_____

24. Based on your answers to questions 22 and 23, what is the **denotation** of the word <u>nonconformist</u>?

24. _____
_____

25. Which one of the four kinds of context clues is given for the underlined word in the following sentence?

His wild <u>gesticulations</u> led the rescuers to him; he waved, jumped up and down energetically, and ran about erratically.

25. _____

Answer Key

Pages 7-9, Pretest
1. Sara
2. third person omniscient
3. the ocean at Kohoa
4. Sara had practiced with caution all week.
5. As Sara tried to stand on her board, she felt a sharp pain.
6. "Sara shook her head as she remembered her own foolishness."
7. anger or rebellion
8. situation
9. strained; determinedly; anger
10. Man versus Man
11. "a sharp pain seized her"
12. "like a mother cat, always overprotecting his athletes"
13. palm trees
14. opinion
15. what the character says (or thinks)
16. what the character does
17. what other characters say about the character
18. A wave caught her board.
19. She cut her ankle.
20. Answers will vary.
21. Both are athletes.
22. Both are headstrong (or determined) people.
23. Coach Jenkins thought that Sara should not compete; Sara thought that she should.
24. Coach Jenkins thought he could stop Sara from competing; Sara knew that he could not.
25. to entertain
26. sky
27. *Synonym*: powerful
28. *Antonym*: weak
29. to stop work
30. Answers will vary.
31. state, condition, quality, or degree of _____
32. again
33. contrast
34. of, relating to, or befitting a child or childhood
35. inappropriate immaturity

Page 10, Climb Aboard
Similarities
1. John Green
2. Columbia Stage Line as agent for Wells, Fargo & Company
3-5. Answers will vary but might include the facts that both tickets are for one passage, and both tickets are for passage from Columbia.
Differences
1. August 15, 1900; July 9, 1868
2. Wichita; Salt Lake
3-5. Answers will vary but might include the following statements:
   One ticket is for coach, and the other is for shotgun.
   One ticket cost $118, and the other cost $96.
   One ticket bears the number 3476, and the other bears the number 2810.

Pages 11-12, "Beleve" It or Not
Facts (Order may vary.)
1. More than one hundred boats and planes have disappeared from the Bermuda Triangle since 1930.
2. History textbooks contain accounts of unexplained disappearances in the Bermuda Triangle.
3. In 1945, Flight 19 vanished in this area.
4. The rescue plane sent to look for Flight 19 also disappeared.
5. In 1881, the *Mary Celeste* was found afloat in this area with no crew aboard and no indication of any disturbance.
6. The Bermuda Triangle is a mystery.
Opinions (Order may vary.)
1. The mystery can be easily explained on the basis of human errors or natural causes.
2. I. Beleve knows better.
3. There is something very mysterious about the waters stretching from Florida to Bermuda to Puerto Rico.
4. The planes were lost as the result of human error.
5. Some wreckage would have been found if the disappearances had natural causes.
6. The unexplained disappearances of boats and planes will never be explained.
7. Clear air turbulence and magnetic variation are not sufficient to explain the continual strange reports coming from that area.
8. The Bermuda Triangle will continue to be a mystery.

Page 16, Just Morse-ing Around
Get ready to send a call for help.
Read about a ship disaster.
Then, on a separate sheet of paper, write a message the ship's radio operator sent just before the ship went down.

Pages 19-20, Make It to the Top
5, 10, 9, 2, 18, 13, 16, 17, 14, 4, 1, 8, 12, 6, 15, 11, 7, 3

Pages 21-22, CPR—A Real Lifesaver
1. Check to be sure that the victim is not breathing and that there is no heartbeat.
2. O 3. E 4. G 5. L 6. D 7. I 8. A 9. C
10. If the heart is beating, continue the breathing technique.
11. K 12. M 13. B 14. H 15. N 16. J 17. F
18. When you detect a pulse, discontinue the pressure-relaxation technique but continue artificial respiration until the victim regains consciousness or help arrives.

Page 24, Strike It Rich
(Order may vary.)
Mining Techniques
1. Panning is the most common technique.
2. "Coyote hole" mining involves digging a shaft and working with a partner and is very dangerous.
Gold Mining Towns
1. lawless
2. expensive
3. wild

Hardships
1. weather
2. back-breaking labor
3. surviving financially until gold is found
4. loneliness

Miners
1. not used to hard work
2. sick
3. sore
4. wild
5. desperate enough to cheat a partner or a friend

Law
1. almost nonexistent
2. Staking a claim consists of marking the claimed area with four pegs, or stakes.
3. Miners' jury makes important legal decisions.

Page 25, Get the Picture?
Answers will vary.

Page 26, Chain of Events
Answers will vary.

Page 27, Keys to Conclusions
1. a. This key would probably open a suitcase or a locker.
   b. It might belong to a flight attendant or a passenger.
2. a. Part of it has been cut off.
   b. It was run over by a train.
3. a. A jewelry box or a diary.
   b. Answers will vary but might include a door.
4. a. One house is old, while the other is new.
   b. The locking mechanism on one door is large, while the locking mechanism on the other door is relatively small.

Pages 28-29, Bills, Bills, Bills
1. He went to Valleyfield, New Hampshire.
2. He bought camping and rock climbing equipment and took climbing lessons.
3. Yes. While trying to climb a mountain, he fell and broke his ankle.
4. He had surgery, used crutches, and received physical therapy.
5. Cleve set out to climb a mountain.
6. Yes, but not as he had originally intended. Instead of climbing, he rode to the top.

Page 30, Fathom This
1. It is a fan-powered wind surfer.
2. On an ocean or a large lake.
3. Because the air was calm, and there was no wind to power it.
4. The surfer stands on a rubber mat (**B**). Two pontoons (**C**) keep the board upright and stable. A battery (**A**) powers the fan (**D**), which creates wind to fill the sail (**E**).
The invention has some problems—obviously!

Page 31, A Majestic Decision
1. Answers will vary.
2. Answers will vary.
3. Intrepid is the leader of their expedition.
4. Probably not.
5. They did not determine their route before the start of the expedition, and they did not bring sufficient supplies to enable them to be flexible enroute.
6. Probably not.
7. They do not seem experienced enough to be able to persuade someone to sponsor them.
8. No.
9. Intrepid's knowledge of the area is based solely on the reports of others.

Page 33, To the Point
1. third person objective
2. third person omniscient
3. third person objective
4. third person objective
5. third person omniscient
6-8. Answers will vary.

Page 39-40, Should You Quote Me?
1. a. inaccurate
   b. what the character says (*or* thinks) and does
   c. "She simply couldn't envision any other life-style that would give her the pleasure and satisfaction she derived from being a test pilot."
2. a. inaccurate
   b. what the character says (*or* thinks)
   c. "'It's funny,' she thought, 'the more dangerous the undertaking, the more I enjoy it.'"
3. a. accurate
   b. what the character says (*or* thinks) and does
   c. assorted statements and descriptions throughout the passage
4. a. accurate
   b. what the character says (*or* thinks) and does
   c. Nancy's perception that no one understands how she feels and her willingness to divorce herself from the feelings of others
5. a. accurate
   b. what the character says (*or* thinks) and does
   c. Nancy immediately dismisses personal concerns when she sees the men waiting for her.
6. a. accurate
   b. what the character says (*or* thinks)
   c. "If only Charles would accept her career commitment and stop his endless efforts to persuade her to do something she didn't want to do and to be something she didn't want to be!"

Page 41, Conflict Connections
1. Man versus Man
2. Man versus Nature
3. This situation contains no apparent conflict.
4. Man versus Society
5. This situation contains no apparent conflict.

6. Man versus Himself
7. Man versus Nature
Rewritten situations will vary.

Page 44, Figure It Out
1. a. The mountain is being compared to a tall building or tower.
   b. This means that the mountain is very high.
2. a. The wave and an angry serpent are being compared.
   b. This means that the wave was twisting and turning, writhing unpredictably like an injured or enraged snake.
3. a. The wind is being compared to an animal that can bite.
   b. The wind is cold and blowing hard. Its touch stings and is as painful as a bite.
4. a. His hand is being compared to a tool used to clamp and hold things securely.
   b. This means that his grip was tight and secure.
   c. This is an effective image because it shows that his hand was grasping the rope very tightly.
5. a. The flower's petals are being compared to tears.
   b. The blossom is losing its petals because summer is ending.
   c. This image conveys a feeling of sorrow at the passing of a season.

Page 45, Figure Eight
1. like a wounded guinea pig
2. fast-footed world title
3. a soggy potato chip
4. as well as peas in a pod
5. like dehydrated aardvarks
6. blaring like a bassoon
7. a chorus of one thousand screeching violins
8. the spotlight pulverized her
Rewritten figures of speech will vary.

Page 48, Forecast the Foreshadowing
1. *Your candle goes out.* There is not enough oxygen in the air to sustain the tiny candle flame. You may have difficulty breathing.
2. *You sense a dark shadow above you.* A plane is flying very close overhead or a fellow sky diver is directly above you. You may need to take some sort of evasive action to avoid a midair collision.
3. *You come across some unspoiled milk.* The house is *not* abandoned, as you had thought. You may discover or be discovered by someone else.
4. *Your guide and all of your bearers have hastily fled.* Something terrifying, of which you are unaware, has frightened them. You may be visited by the same terrifying something, or you may simply have to face the problems associated with being in the jungle alone.
5. *You hear a series of thuds on the deck.* Either an uninvited guest has joined you, or your equipment has failed. You may need to cope with company, repair your equipment, or pray for rescue.

6. *You find a large box.* Someone knows your secret and has planted a bomb to gain revenge. You must decide whether to disarm the device yourself or to call for help at the risk of having to reveal your identity.
7. *The falling snow has obliterated your tracks.* Unless you have carefully made mental note of some particular landmarks, you are probably lost. You must now dig in to withstand the snowstorm and hope for eventual rescue.
8. *You notice a shoelace beginning to trail.* Your shoelace has come untied, and you are likely to trip on it unless you retie it. You must decide whether to continue running at the risk of falling or to take time to tie your shoelace at the risk of losing the race.
9. *Your companion is nowhere in sight.* Your companion has disappeared and may have slipped down the precipice. You must decide whether or not to risk your own life by searching for him or her.
10. *You suddenly notice a smooth, V-shaped section of water.* There is a obstacle in the water. You must decide how to maneuver safely around it.

Page 49, Foreshadowing Forecast: Danger Ahead!
Answers will vary.

Pages 50-51, Mood Messages
I. Setting
1. "The roar of a lion thundered through the nearby woods."
2. Answers will vary.
II. Description
1. "Light, sparkling snowflakes wafted past him."
2. Answers will vary.
III. Situation
1. The majority of the sentences in this paragraph work together to create a mood of apprehension, fear, and desperation.
2. *Circled words:* desperately clutching, grabbed, push aside, pelted
3. "Her thoughts drifted happily to the sun and fun she had expected."
4. Answers will vary.

Page 52, Focus on the Setting
1. a. the present
   b. underwater
2. a. midday
   b. a jungle
3. a. the future
   b. the launchpad for a flying saucer or other similar space vehicle
4. a. early evening
   b. a mountain peak

Page 56, Safari Strain
1. *Underlined words:* satisfactory; annoyed; her usual lack of control
   Tone: disappointed annoyance

2. *Underlined words:* usual assortment of middle-aged, overweight, and out-of-shape passengers; hearing damage; I had no idea a human being could sustain a scream for five solid minutes; You'll come to know and love Mr. Smith; his possessions are scattered all over East Africa.
Tone: patronizingly humorous

3. *Underlined words:* dusty, shaken, exhausted; This is fun? I tried to tell George that a safari wouldn't be all he had hoped; death-defying; furious; terrifying
Tone: long-suffering tolerance

Pages 59-66, An Undersea Adventure with a Twist
Introduction
1. The setting of this story is the present, near a coral reef.
2. Lucas is the main character.
3. He is engaged in skin diving and underwater photography.
4. Man versus Himself
5. when Lucas remembers Rick's warning
6. to emphasize the element of danger inherent in skin diving, especially alone
7. "stab of concern" and "He'd just have to be especially careful."

Episode A
1. *Circled words:* sea anemones beckoned gently
2. iridescent shapes; silent clicks
3. *Underlined statement:* Lucas smiled to himself.

Episode B
1. third person omniscient
2. *Circled clues:* fish suddenly became agitated and moved quickly away; menacing black shape

Episode C
1. He is an unrealistic dreamer, and he is reckless, or impulsive.
2. what the character does and what the author says about the character

Episode D
1. Man versus Himself
2. When faced with a choice between retreating from and staying in a potentially dangerous situation, Lucas decides to stay.

Episode E
1. The mood is one of anxiety or apprehension.
2. The mood is created primarily by situation.

Episode F
1. a boat
2. *Clues:* triangular form; churning propeller blade

Episode G
1. The 18 symbolizes fortune and discovery.
2. The theme of this story is perseverance and realization of a dream.
3. If the object had proved to be merely a piece of rusty metal, the theme would have been that dreams do not always come true no matter how hard you work or how long you persevere.

Episode H
1. The tone is tongue-in-cheek.
2. No, it has varied from episode to episode.

Episode I
1. The theme of the story is that persistent effort pays off or is rewarded.
2. Answers will vary.
3. Answers will vary.

Episode J
1. Discretion is the better part of valor.
2. Yes.
3. Lucas has shown himself to be reckless and impulsive; however, his decision to retreat shows caution and good judgment.

Episode K
1. A moral is a practical lesson that can be drawn from a story.
2. A moral is a lesson that can be drawn from a story; a theme is the subject, topic, or underlying idea of the story.
3. Always follow the advice of those who are wiser than you are.

Episode L
1. *Circled simile:* performed like a vaudeville-hall ham
2. This simile means that the animal acted like a person who enjoys performing on stage for an audience.

Episode M
1. The tone is ironic
2. Yes.
3. The mood is cynical.
4. No, it differs. Previously, the mood had been one of anxiety or apprehension.

Episode N
1. Lucas has a great deal of pride.
2. Sensory details include the pounding of Lucas's heart and the opening and closing of his mouth in silent cries for help.
3. The tone is ironic.

Page 67, Consider the Connotations
Positive Connotation
1. remodeled   2. lofty   3. challenging   4. lush
5. remote   6. romantic   7. exotic   8. spacious
9. heirlooms   10. painstakingly   11. peaceful
12. perpetually   13. leisurely   14. unspoiled
15. balmy
Negative Connotation
1. patched up   2. imposing   3. death-defying
4. wild   5. isolated   6. sappy   7. strange
8. cavernous   9. pink   10. cautiously   11. dull
12. incessantly   13. slow   14. primitive   15. bland

Page 68, A "Remoat" Vacation
1. remodeled   2. lofty   3. challenging
4. unspoiled   5. lush   6. remote   7. romantic
8. spacious   9. heirlooms   10. exotic
11. painstakingly   12. leisurely   13. peaceful
14. balmy   15. perpetually

Page 69, Do You "Sea" the Analogy?
1. road map   2. storm   3. pilot   4. land
5. surveyor   6. pressure   7. star   8. astronaut
9. forest   10. stern

Answer Key
(continued)

Page 70, Contest Cavern
Answers will vary.

Page 71, Crafty Clues
1. sparcebur   2. zodaf   3. blipstig   4. drastig
5. mordeldow   6. listermat   7. sleever   8. crosbean
9. froster   10. zurup   11. breden   12. burneystig
13. waterwam   14. schloodle   15. sooley   16. brarney

Page 72, Jungle Trackdown
Descriptions may vary and should, where possible, be more detailed.
1. a climbing herbaceous vine
2. a bright-colored tropical fish that swims in schools and often attacks and inflicts dangerous wounds upon men and large animals
3. a tropical ungulate related to the horse
4. a large arboreal game bird
5. a South American game bird
6. a tropical American tree of the trumpet-creeper family
7. a large, extremely venomous pit viper
8. a Central and South American crocodilian
9. a palm
10. a heron
11. a large, semiaquatic snake
12. a mammal that inhabits tropical forests
13. a tropical American pit viper
14. a parrot of Central and South America
15. a tropical American mammal related to the raccoon but having a longer body and tail and a long, flexible snout.

Plants: buriti, calabash, liana
Fish: piranha
Birds: bittern, curassow, macaw, tinamou
Reptiles: anaconda, bushmaster, caiman, fer-de-lance
Mammals: coati, sloth, tapir

Page 73, Homonym Hang-up
Answers will vary.

Page 74, Hang in There
Sentences will vary.

Page 75, The Etymology Express
Answers will vary but might include some of the following words: active, actor, agreeable, careful, conform, deplane, disagree, disagreeable, export, fairly, inform, information, informative, interview, merger, mistrust, notable, notary, payable, payment, postdate, predate, prescribe, prescription, react, reform, report, reporter, submerge, subscribe, subscription, transcribe, transcription, transport, transportation, tricycle, tricyclist, unfair, unfairly, unicycle, unicyclist

Page 76, Cast About for a Synonym
1. taciturn   2. wistful   3. indigent   4. optimistic
5. defiant   6. indomitable   7. enigmatic
8. audacious   9. apathetic   10. vacillating
11. affluent   12. enterprising   13. poignant
14. lethargic   15. rakish

Page 77, Pack a Thesaurus
1. Sentinel   2. chasm   3. traversed   4. alpinist
5. hazards   6. incline   7. sheer   8. enterprising
9. bravado   10. citadel   11. pinnacle   12. tribute

Page 78, How's That Again, Pardner?
1. Stick 'em up!
2. Head 'em off at the pass.
3. Take cover! It's an ambush!
4. They'll never take me alive.
5. There's gold in them thar hills.
6. Reach for the sky.
7. It's a bad day at Black Rock.
8. It's good to be back home on the range again.
9. We're surrounded!
10. Go west, young man.

Page 87, Caution—Misplaced Modifier Ahead!
1. Carrying a parachute, the sky diver leaped from the top of the tall building.
2. While rappelling from a mountain peak, the climber discovered a hidden cave.
3. Dazed by the unrelenting sun, the hunters sought shelter beneath a tree.
4. While sitting by the campfire, the explorers examined the map.
5. While shooting through the rapids, the canoe hit a rock.

Page 88, Action Adverbs
Answers will vary.

Page 93, Hunt a Word
Underlined words: danger, extend, motion, rescue, travel
Other answers will vary.

Page 96, Good News/Bad News
Answers will vary but should follow the pattern set by the examples.

Page 97, Shades-of-Meaning Spectra
Answers will vary but should follow the pattern set by the example.

Pages 104-107, Shoot for the Stars!
1-17. Answers will vary.
18. shelter
19. hazardous; unstable; doubtful; delicate; sensitive
20. bold; brave
21. an unexpected period of uninterrupted or repeated demand
22. together; with
23. one who performs an action or makes a (specified) thing
24. one who does not form with or in harmony to; one who does not adapt to the people around him or to the situation in which he finds himself
25. example